Management for Professionals

The Springer series *Management for Professionals* comprises high-level business and management books for executives. The authors are experienced business professionals and renowned professors who combine scientific background, best practice, and entrepreneurial vision to provide powerful insights into how to achieve business excellence.

More information about this series at http://www.springer.com/series/10101

Dan Norenberg

Executive Ownershift

Creating Highly Effective Leadership Teams

Springer

Dan Norenberg
Munich, Germany

ISSN 2192-8096 ISSN 2192-810X (electronic)
Management for Professionals
ISBN 978-3-030-35827-3 ISBN 978-3-030-35828-0 (eBook)
https://doi.org/10.1007/978-3-030-35828-0

This Springer imprint is published by the registered company Springer Nature Switzerland AG
The registered company address is: Gewerbestrasse 11, 6330 Cham, Switzerland

Foreword

Few of us fail to realize how important leadership is to the quality of our lives and the success of our businesses. I have spent most of my adult life helping many of the world's most successful leaders become even more successful. Throughout these wonderful experiences, I have learned that change, improvement and growth never stop for leaders who are committed to playing at their best.

Yet as we see in sports, music and business, the contributions and results created by a star contributor do not alone guarantee team effectiveness, a championship or business success.

Yet leadership, for far too many, is still seen and practiced as a solo endeavor. The myth of the heroic leader still exists for many, who believe that a team, an orchestra or an organization's success is determined by the magic of one.

It is the combined effort of all the members of a leadership team, from which we can measure the success they bring to their organization, to their customers and their markets.

I learned years ago that no matter how good each of us is, we can and will get better if we invite and utilize the people around us to help us improve. These people see us at our best, and our worst, and are nearly always interested in seeing us succeed. This is the foundation of my executive coaching practice, called Stakeholder Centered Coaching®. Executives that work with me are required to seek regular feedback, or as I say, feedforward suggestions for continuous improvement, and my clients have made remarkable improvements because of their commitments to this process.

Dan Norenberg and I initially connected through my Stakeholder Centered Coaching© program, as he is one of our certified coaches. Dan is also a member of my 100 European Coaches Program that we started this past Spring at the Henley Business School near London. The 100 Coaches Europe program recognizes exceptional coaches and contributors to the field of professional leadership development.

Dan has brought something more to our coaching community, namely his transformational growth process for leadership teams, called Executive Ownershift®.

Dan's work (and his book) focuses on the leadership team, as it is the moral and performance barometer of the organization. In Dan's words, change, improvement and growth start at the top of the organization, not the middle or the bottom of the organization. True leadership development works best when the entire team learns together, thus creating accountability among the team members for their growth. This also sets the example for the personal nature and priority that senior leadership teams place on change, and that it starts with them.

I appreciate Dan's work because he shares his deeply personal experiences from life and leadership teams, his keen observations and interventions with over 100 senior leadership teams, as well as a framework for continuous improvement that every leadership team can use to grow themselves and their business.

You can read Executive Ownershift® from cover to cover, as a reference guide, or go directly to the area where your teams need help most. It is full of personal stories, metaphors and pragmatic tools to help your leadership team play at its best. In Dan's words, when leadership teams play at their best, everyone in your organization has a better opportunity to play at their best.

My forty plus years as an executive coach has brought me into contact with exciting leaders, creative coaches and novel ideas to help us all improve. Dan Norenberg and his book, Executive Ownershift®, is something I can recommend to leaders who recognize that their leadership team is a growth generator for the entire business.

Above all things, remember that life is good.

With Regards
Marshall Goldsmith
Best Selling Author, *Triggers & What Got You Here Won't Get You There*
Thinkers50 "World's Most Influential Leadership Thinker"
Inc. Magazine "America's #1 Executive Coach"

Rancho Santa Fe, CA, USA
July 2019

Acknowledgements

This book is intended to serve and support those who believe that leadership teams are everything to the success of their organization.

In this light, I am grateful to the hundreds, perhaps thousands, of leaders that have trusted me to help them on their growth journey as professionals. Specifically, I would like to thank Amer Ahmed, Ervin Appelfeld, Dietrich Fechner, Lars Henrikson, Jacques Richier and Frank Wiemer, all who set aside valuable time to make personal contributions to this work.

Dr. Yury Boshyk, Dr. Marshall Goldsmith and Dr. Alan Weiss are each profoundly intelligent thought leaders in their respective fields. I have been extremely fortunate to have learned so much from these three superb mentors.

Jerry O'Brien's skill and watchful eye over the course of this project helped my writing a great deal, and Paul Rulkens gave his valuable time to review the manuscript, so to both of you, a huge thanks. A special thanks to Nicholas Jack, at Jack Media, for providing the graphics and visualizations at various points throughout this book.

Lastly, to my family, Uta, Noah and Lea; I am deeply grateful for your never-ending understanding and patience throughout this writing experience. You bring so much light and love to my life that I cannot help but to step forward each day in the most joyful way.

Introduction

I have advised, coached and consulted with leaders and their organizations on three continents over the past 25 years, from the shop floor to the executive suite, with thousands of profound stops in between. This book looks deeply into my experiences with executive teams, the people and businesses they lead.

Yet *another* book on leadership, you may be thinking…

While it is true that much has been written and even more talked about regarding what effective leadership is and how to make it happen, we must be honest with ourselves.

The leadership playing field has dramatically changed over the past 30 years, and while more executive coaches, business schools, leadership models and diagnostic instruments promise to have the "next best thing", we must ask ourselves:

Why are high performing executive teams so rare?

Even in leadership teams with natural talent, huge amounts of intellectual firepower and an abundance of ambition, we see organizations that struggle to create a highly engaged workforce, a compelling strategy and exceptional, sustainable results over time.

I believe that we stand at a leadership crossroad. In one direction, the road sign says, continue in this way for more of the same. It is predictable and let me say, the status quo road that is frequently traveled. There is another road sign that says, challenging road ahead, potential hazards and struggles, with remarkable destinations along the way.

This book is a guide and map to the second road, the challenging road with potential hazards, struggles and remarkable destinations. I deeply believe that we must help leaders now to take a different road and this is why I have written this book.

I have worked closely with over 100 senior leadership teams. These experiences, through intimate work with senior teams who strive to get it right and learn from what goes wrong, have helped me shape a transformational leadership growth process that is different from what mainstream leadership consultants and the majority of organizations practice today. My approach and leadership practice, that I call Executive Ownershift®, are anchored in three principles:

Leadership is a Team Endeavor

Most organizations and mainstream consultants see leadership as an individual endeavor. This is not the most effective approach because your company's success depends on the effective teamwork and collaboration of your leaders, not their individual talents. An executive team is often a collection of highly talented and experienced leaders, but rarely functions as a highly effective team. Yet these leadership teams are the organic engines of growth and deserve the opportunity to develop and improve as a team and not simply as a fragmented collection of individual leaders. At the heart of Executive Ownershift, leadership is a team endeavor.

Leadership (Development) is Top Down, Not Bottom Up

Far too often, people's improvement and growth are addressed "bottom up," because senior leaders are too busy with other issues, think they are already good enough or are reluctant to address their challenges publicly. This cannot be the example that leads to an organization performing at its best. If you want to change your business, leaders must change themselves. You can only improve and grow your business when leaders improve and grow. This should not start at the bottom of your organization; it should start at the top. From my experience, executives that have the courage and discipline to share that growth and improvement begins with them and then follow through create strong emotional bonds with people who are eager to follow such an example.

Exceptional Leadership Teams Practice the Lincoln Law

Abraham Lincoln was the quintessential self-made man. This meant diligence, active development and self-education. Never did he see himself as a "finished product," even as President of the USA. Lincoln once wrote to his law partner, William Herndon, who asked advice about how to succeed. "The way (for a young man) to rise is to improve himself every way he can" [1]. The surest way to succeed, from Lincoln's perspective, was to improve himself, not expect others to change.

Others call this the oxygen mask rule [2]. You must first help yourself, as instructed by the airlines, before you can help anyone else. When you are part of a leadership team, it is critical that you and your executive team members decide how you are going to help yourselves before you jump in to help others. Executives are confronted from day one with a multitude of problems to solve and opportunities to address. Everyone wants something from senior executives; this is where many executive teams make the mistake of jumping into their company's business issues too deeply at the beginning of their team's evolution.

This fast start often means a fractional start, because leadership teams do not spend enough time, nor create the right structures for their team to perform at its best. Moreover, once they surround themselves with company issues, they have little time, patience or energy to address the practices required to become a high-performance executive team.

Through my work, I am convinced that helping leadership teams play at their best remains the single most valuable investment an organization can make if they want to become a first-class performer.

This calling to work with leadership teams is more than a job or an occupation for me; this is the thing I was born to do. Through my many years of experience in this field, I have seen a multitude of leadership initiatives, all started with the best of intentions. Yet the vast majority of them overlooked the importance of helping *leaders, as a team, to play at their best.*

Leadership team success never appears in isolation. In other words, when your leadership team performs well, so do others and vice versa. I had never encountered a high-performance organization run by a failing leadership team. Conversely, I had not experienced a highly effective leadership team that sat on top of a lackluster organization. Their mutual success, or failure, goes hand in hand.

You do not need legions of consultants to improve your business. I believe that leadership teams (when given the space, time and disruptive growth practices) can transform their own business. We should not rob leadership teams of the opportunity to create their own breakthroughs. Results come fast to executive teams that recognize that they are the starting point for improvement and growth. This enables struggling leadership teams to become good and good leadership teams to become great.

If you are an executive leader, I trust you will find this book a helpful resource for you and your team. If you support leadership development or aspire to grow into an executive leadership position, this book can accelerate your growth through the experiences, practices and tools described. Even if you do not aspire to become a member of an executive leadership team, I am confident that you will take useful ideas from this resource. Leadership development is a personal development, and after all, is not that why we are here?

Executive Ownershift® is both serious work and serious play. Both head and heart works are required to make it work for your team. The first steps of *Ownershift* come with the realization that our performance could be so much more and the personal courage to step forward and say *there is work to do (and potential to be exploited) and it starts with me and my leadership team.*

If at times it seems that I take a critical view of executive teams and their shortcomings, it is because at the executive level, the tone and tempo of an effective consultant or advisor differ from that of someone working at other levels of the organization. The last thing executives need are diplomatic niceties or an overabundance of compliments heaped on them. Executives consistently tell me that the frank and pointed feedback I give them is a welcomed difference to the fuzzy and diplomatic language they often get from the people around them.

I continue to be "constructively challenged" through my work with executives who aspire to lead better teams and better businesses. I am humbled and continuously learning from them. They have given me permission to coach and support their continued pursuit of excellence, yet I draw infinitely from their expertise, ambition and the creative desire to develop a better organization than the one they inherited. For this, I am most grateful.

Let me mention that the examples I share come from my experiences with leaders and their teams. At times, the names and specific details have been changed to respect the intimate permission and trust that these executive teams gave to me. I am deeply appreciative of their willingness to move into the unknown, so all of us can learn to become better leaders and create better leadership teams.

If at the end of this book you have been inspired, challenged, gained a new perspective or taken just one idea that you can use for your executive team or in your personal life, then this has been a worthwhile endeavor.

Enjoy the experience!

Munich, Germany
July 2019

Dan Norenberg
CEO, Catalyst for Executive Ownershift

References

1. Winkle, K. (Summer 2000) Abraham Lincoln: Self made man. United States. *Journal of the Abraham Lincoln Association*, *21*(2). https://quod.lib.umich.edu/j/jala/2629860.0021.203/–abraham-lincoln-self-made-man?rgn=main;view=fulltext.
2. Pausch, R., & Zaslow, J. (2008) *The last lecture*. New York: Hyperion Publishing.

Contents

1 Cracks in the Leader's Ship

Failure is not fatal, but failure to change is.

1.1 Vulnerability

"Is coach home?"

I am ten years old and just opened the front door. It is pouring rain and a huge man is standing on the front porch, bent over and sopping wet.

He asks again, "Is coach home?"

I run back to the kitchen table where we are eating dinner and tell Dad that some man is standing on our front porch. Dad goes to the door.

While Dad takes him into the living room, Mom puts the coffee pot on and I hear muffled voices and an occasional light crying from someone who must truly be in a lot of pain.

Sometime later, Dad walks out with him, he is standing straighter, they shake hands and he disappears into the dark night.

At breakfast the next morning, I ask Dad who stopped by last night and what was going on.

Dad said that was *so and so*, and he stopped by last night to talk.

"That was *so and so*", I said excitedly. "He played football for you, he was first team all-conference, got all state honors when he played for you. He did not look so good last night", I finished.

Dad turned to me and said, "Sometimes, life gives us a bit more than we can handle. People deal with this in different ways, some run away from it, some drown it in drink, some take it out on others and some people have the courage to simply say, "This is too much for me right now and ask for help. There is nothing wrong with asking for help; we all need help from time to time and people that recognize that they are in trouble and ask for help usually get themselves turned around pretty quickly".

D. Norenberg, *Executive Ownershift*, Management for Professionals,
https://doi.org/10.1007/978-3-030-35828-0_1

It took me years before I understood what my Dad meant. Strength comes, with the ability to share weakness.

Leaders that are unable or unwilling to express their vulnerability, especially within their leadership team, struggle to master the massive challenges that they face. As a leader, if you are really striving to play at your best, at some point you are going to struggle.

Yet if you hold the internal belief that asking for help is a weakness, you will not reach out and get the help you need to move through whatever challenge you are facing. When leaders confuse vulnerability with incompetence or helplessness, they overcompensate and hide or disguise their vulnerability. By attempting to appear strong, you actually become weaker.

As a leadership team, the cost of not expressing vulnerability compounds itself because those around you mirror what you do and what you say. When you are not asking for help, people that report to you will not either. When people feel that they have to manage everything on their own, or risk being seen as weak or helpless, everyone struggles.

Consider how a "low expressed vulnerability" influences a leadership team's strategic business review. Most leadership teams review their strategic progress, comparing what they aspire to do with what is actually happening. What is happening or not happening in your strategic review sessions? Do you experience strong expressions of vulnerability, or not, in your strategic reviews? Some do, most do not.

Many strategic reviews are really a masquerade party, where leaders put on their professional mask and try to show that things are going well, when often they are not.

People do not ask tough questions, thinking, "If I dig into his business critically, he might do the same to me," and people begin to practice friendly avoidance, steering clear of the obstacles that might be blocking success. Few leaders stand up and say, "I am uncertain how to engage with my team on this new initiative, can anyone help me?"

Simply because a strategic review is full of slides and content, does not make it rich in vulnerability, yet the latter is where we can help others, learn and improve.

If everyone was as good as they say they are during strategic reviews; why do so few organizations meet or exceed their strategic objectives?

This can also spread beyond the leadership team and become institutionalized. Your company could suffer from a lack of organizational vulnerability. Naturally, you do not leave your company doors unlocked all night, allow sloppy procedures in your clean rooms, or put your company at risk with half-hearted due diligence activities.

These are not good places to be vulnerable as an organization.

Organizational vulnerability means trust runs deep through your organization. You can measure this by the degree that people are encouraged to take risks and make choices of their own accord.

How does your organization show it trusts the people that work there?

Does your organization express its vulnerability, meaning it trusts people to make choices about:

- Business travel arrangements?
- Hiring people?
- Investing in growth areas?
- Attending relevant activities and events outside the company?

In some organizations, the official word is, we trust you, but through their actions, they say, we do not really trust you and in fact, if you want something, you have to go up three levels in the organization to get approval because the reality is; trust is reserved for a very select few here.

Over time, a company that does not express some vulnerability towards the people that work there will destroy itself, or at best become insignificant, because real performers will not want to play ball with them.

It is hard to become a chess player if you feel like a chess piece.

If you take risk taking out of leadership, you create a culture of clones. Clones never develop a sense of ownership; instead feel an obligation to merely execute. This feeling of obligation does not lead to discretionary effort, the secret sauce created in ownership cultures.

Just because you lock up your business at night does not mean that you cannot keep open the doors that lead to a culture of ownership; it starts with exploring how you practice organizational vulnerability.

Leaders who express vulnerability as a positive and necessary leadership characteristic invite openness, sensitivity and demonstrate self-confidence within their team; this can be a real game changer. It reminds us, and those around us, that we are authentic, and above all human. When you know, and can publicly share, what you do not know or you cannot do, you can learn it.

These first steps of *ownershift* come with the realization that no matter who we are, or what position we have achieved, there is always room to change, improve and grow our performance. With this belief, coupled with a willingness to share vulnerability, shows personal courage to step forward and say *there is work to do (and potential to be exploited) and it starts with me and my leadership team.*

I have witnessed first-hand the power that expressing vulnerability, and encouraging others to do the same, has on leadership teams who strive to lead at their best. Vulnerability is a sign of courage and authenticity, both vital characteristics for effective leadership. How does vulnerability show up in your leadership team? Do courageous and authentic conversations take place amongst team members?

Reflect on these questions to help you become more aware, more expressive and supportive of vulnerability in yourself and within your leadership team:

Where am I vulnerable, and in what ways do I express this to others?
How and where do I ask for help?
How do I model the way for my direct reports to express their vulnerabilities?
To what degree do I understand the vulnerabilities of my leadership colleagues?
In what way do we support each other when someone shares they are struggling, in trouble or in search of a good idea?

Even in positions of great power, the ability to recognize and learn from our own human limitations can accelerate our leadership effectiveness. Julian Zeilzer summed it up well when he said, "Great presidents are aware of their own limitations and capable of learning from their mistakes. This is an essential quality of effective leadership, otherwise the person in power is unable to grow and incapable of bouncing back from moments of political peril." [1].

I will be forever grateful to the man (and the many others), who showed up from time to time on our front porch. They were able to express their vulnerability, coming forward when they thought they could not bear any more burden. They gave me a valuable insight and a critically important characteristic in the executive ownershift process.

1.2 The Cobbler's Children Go Barefoot

This is an insightful proverb, dating back over five hundred years. It is a saying that indicates how some professionals do not apply their skills to themselves. We see the proverb in different forms, doctors are the worst patients is another example, and it is highly relevant for executive teams that say they want to play at their best. It reminds me of the following situation.

Dominque was excited and highly motivated for me to meet with her boss, President of European Operations. The company had gone through a time consuming business integration, leadership teams across Europe were not performing well, customer satisfaction was down due to late delivery of their technology related products and executive leadership was looking for a way to turn their situation around.

As senior VP of Human Resources, Dominique was business driven and results oriented. She was impressed with my experience and track record of working with senior leadership teams. We had had a number of meetings to discuss her company's situation and now it was time to talk with Richard, President of the business.

After a round of introductions and after reaching a common understanding of their current situation, Richard asked me how my approach to business excellence could support their turnaround.

After introducing my approach, underlining that change, improvement and growth for the business starts with the executive team, he interrupted me and turned to Dominque and asked, "You're not thinking of this approach for our executive team, are you?"

There was an awkward moment of silence, Dominque's positive composure changed and she said unevenly, "Well, no, not actually with our senior executive team, but I thought this approach could be helpful for some of the country leaders and their teams because many of them are really struggling."

The meeting continued for another 30 min, but it was a struggle, because we were not really at the heart of the issue. Although I attempted to share that improvement and growth initiatives bring significant gains by starting with the executive leadership team, Richard had made up his mind and drawn his line in the sand. The line in the sand said, "We need something, but it's not going to start with us."

This was unfortunate, as Dominque had previously shared with me that Richard was a good person to work for, highly intelligent, engineering driven and committed to the business yet he could not see or would not accept that his leadership team was not playing at its best, which it was not.

Like the cobbler, who does not see that only his children do not have shoes, executive leadership teams that fail to put themselves under the critical lens of continuous improvement miss the opportunity to grow, improve and as important, own the transformation they so often ask of others.

I have yet to meet the perfect executive team, one that has no room for improvement. Yet only a small percentage of executive teams commit to a systematic development process for themselves. We see sporadic development, but too often, it is focused on individual leader development, and not often enough on leadership development, that challenges the entire team to step up their game. It is only on the leadership team level that development initiatives can bring improved leadership performance and renewed organizational results.

An exceptional executive coaching approach worth mentioning is the outstanding work done by Dr. Marshall Goldsmith and his organization. His innovative approach to coaching executives is called Stakeholder Centered Coaching® and involves the key stakeholders of the executive being coached to serve as accountability partners. This enables those closest to the executive to support and give feedback to them to sustain the desired behaviorial changes the executive aspires to make [2]. Marshall's approach to executive coaching is very effective, and I am proud to be a certified Stakeholder Centered Coach® in his organization.

When I began working with executive teams, I initially saw myself as a missionary out to convert non-believers as to the value and potential benefits of a team approach to leadership and organizational growth. Although the results and client feedback have confirmed my beliefs, today my strategy is more about attraction than conversion. This means that vital to potential engagement with a client, the senior leader must own the belief that improving and growing their business starts with them, personally and secondly with his or her executive leadership team. The executive team does not need to be convinced, at this point, but the senior ranking leader must.

Here are the signs of a resistant executive or resistant executive team:

- Blaming predecessors for the current state of the business
- Point to competitors and complain that they are competing unfairly
- Ignore problem areas in the business (often can be traced back to the leadership team) and point to other successes
- Speaking badly about a part of the business (that's not performing) and not taking ownership for the problems at the executive level
- Surround themselves with people who support their beliefs and who won't challenge the current state of the business

– Accuse people of being negative and pessimistic, without really looking for evidence that supports the challenges people are making.

Sometimes a senior executive leader says to me, "Dan this approach sounds interesting and potentially helpful to us, come in and present this to our executive team and if they like it, we go ahead with you."

In these instances, I point out that the decision to take action and enable the senior leadership team to play at their best rests with the senior executive of the team, not the team itself. This is authority and a decision that cannot be delegated to the team. An executive that is unable or unwilling to lead the way or own the decision to engage in this process would not be an appropriate candidate for Executive Ownershift.

An executive that cannot make or will not make such a decision on behalf of his or her team is not leading a team, they are leading a committee where everyone has a say in everything. (More about committees in Chap. 5.) In my work, the "go ahead signal" is when the senior executive decides to go forward with such a process. I point out that while the decision to go or not go rests with the senior executive, what themes and potential outcomes our work together should address most certainly involves members of the executive team, as this become the fuel for the future executive agenda.

1.3 What Does "Pretty Good" Leadership Mean?

"How is your executive leadership team performing?"

I bring this question to the initial conversation with a leader that is interested in working with me. I listen to the content of the executive's answer, and as important is how they answer the question, meaning I am listening for emotional attachment and rational justifications that may come with their responses. For example:

"We're getting along and seem to be managing the business. There are a lot of different characters in this team so we can't expect them to really get along that well." This could imply, *we do not work well together and I do not want to get in the middle of this, maybe it will get better on its own.*

"Our leadership team is doing well, it's the next level below where the breakdown begins and we start to get in trouble." This could signify, *we are not owning up to our part of this breakdown, somebody's at fault but it is not my team.*

"We are pretty good, all things considered." This could mean, *we do not have any burning fires; we are comfortable and see no sense of urgency at the moment.*

Prior to this question about their leadership team, we've discussed the business, where it's at and where it's going, successes and challenges and now I am going to help this executive look at the link between what is happening (or not) in their business and how it is connected to the leadership team performance.

To understand the picture this senior executive has of their team, and to explore growth potential in the team; I ask how many of the following statements that they strongly agree with, as it relates to their senior leadership team, and to give one concrete example:

(1) High performance and exceptional results in our business can be directly linked to the effectiveness of our executive team.
(2) The leadership behaviors in our executive team excite and engage people in our organization.
(3) Our executive team collaborates and supports each other in such a way that it sets the positive example for others in our company.
(4) Our executive team leads the most effective meetings in our company.
(5) Our business strategy is clear and emotionally compelling, due to the effort and example set by the executive team.
(6) Our executive leadership team is playing at its best.

These statements help an executive look at how their business is performing and the connection this performance has to the senior leadership team. With new insights that the executive has developed over the course of our conversation, we can move the last statement into a question:

"Are you and your Executive Leadership Team really playing at your best?"

Moreover, their response is always, "Well, if I am really honest, and look at our team critically, we're not playing at our best."

"If you and your executive team are playing at less than your best, what does this cost your business (missed market opportunities, little sense of urgency and engagement, ad hoc strategic execution), and how can you expect anyone else in this company to play at their best", I ask?

In my experience, and as I mentioned in the introduction, organization structures, processes or strategy are often blamed when a company is not performing well. You can change the structures, the processes and even the strategy, but if people do not change, you will always have more of the same. If you always do what you have always done, you will always get what you always got, regardless of cosmetic shifting.

When the executive team owns up to the fact that what is happening in their business originates with them, the Executive Ownershift process starts to take hold. A sense of urgency grows when the leadership teams recognizes and takes ownership for the consequences that "pretty good leadership" has for the rest of their organization. Their words and their actions become steps towards positive transformation.

1.4 What Is the Cost of that Crack?

Leadership teams that understand how they influence the direction, speed and collaboration throughout their organization are eager to improve their game, individually and collectively as they know it has a direct correlation on their company's performance. Here are three principles that serve as a gentle reminder that change and improvement begin at the top of the organization, namely the senior leadership team.

Field of Consequences

It is often not clear or not deeply discussed how the actions in the leadership team (or lack of actions) influence the rest of the organization. From my experience, the ability to recognize how the operations of the executive team affect the organization (for better or for worse) is a capability often found in high performance leadership teams. Leadership teams that struggle do not make this connection.

For example, when I ask senior executives if their leadership meeting is the most effective meeting in the company, only a few hands acknowledge that it is. Imagine a poorly run executive meeting. How many meetings take place in their organization every day? Hundreds, thousands perhaps. This is an easy place to go for improvement and growth. The way we do anything is the way we do everything and your company's culture is directly related to the tone, tempo and results created in your executive leadership meeting.

Taking ownership for the field of consequences created by the executive team is a distinction of highly effective leadership teams. The field of consequences, see Fig. 1.1, shows that the higher in the organization you are, the broader the consequences of your actions are felt in the organization.

Let us look at a couple examples. At the IC or individual contributor level, if someone makes a mistake or does a bad job, the damage done is limited to their scope, which is less than a bad job or mistake at the strategic leadership level. Here the field of influence is far greater, and the effect more profound. At the executive level, the field of consequence encompasses the entire organization. This why football teams often exchange the head coach, as they are seen as having the highest field of consequence on the team. Leaders that learn to examine their actions, decisions and peer relationships with the field of consequences in mind operate more thoughtfully and deliberately.

Performance Half-Life

Pretty good leadership at the executive level can have devastating results when viewed through the perspective called performance half-life. Think of sunlight, penetrating layers of water in the ocean and how the further you move from the surface, the less light that gets through. If at the executive level, your "performance sunlight" is only "pretty bright", you will not get light penetration at the lower levels like you would if your executive team were shining brightly.

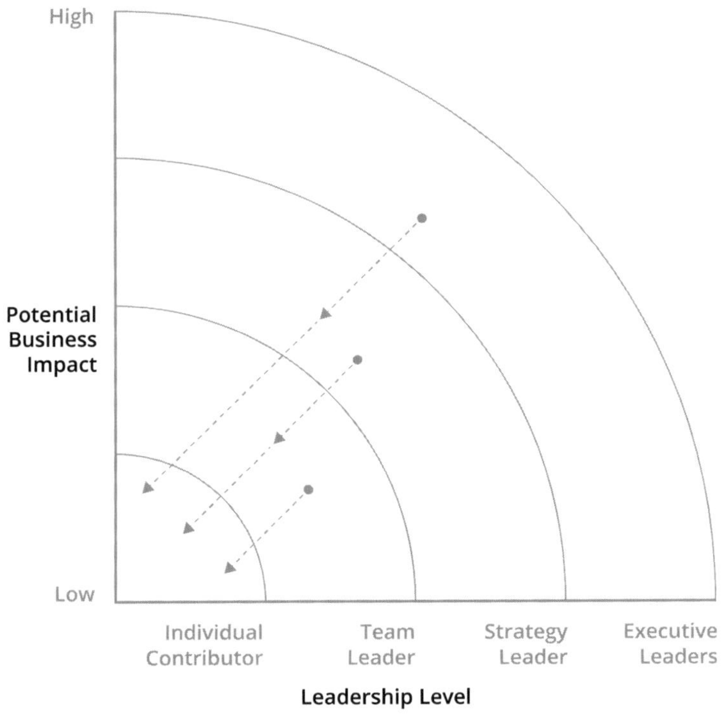

Fig. 1.1 Field of consequences

Given numerical values, it would look like this:

Say that you rate your leadership team performance at a "7" out of "10"; and you consider that pretty good. The performance at the next level down in the organization, in most cases, performs lower than the level above them, usually 25% to 30% less. In addition, the level below them is going to perform even lower, again about 25% less. Therefore, when you say that your leadership team is pretty good, three levels down in your organization, you are at best operating at 3 or 4. This is not only demotivating for employees; it is a level of performance that puts your business at risk. Self-inflicted risk by being complacent with "a pretty good executive team".

Performance Source Codes

When something is not working well in your organization, it is essential that the leadership team locates the *performance source code* (PSC) of this issue, meaning the link back into the senior leadership team. Like the computer program that operates from a "master script" and cannot deviate from this script or source code, so too is the performance source code of your organization.

Often problems are "fixed" at the end of the performance source code chain, yet the origin or original script that leads to the problem is seldom examined, more rarely followed into the executive environment. This is why similar problems pop up over and over, because they are not addressed at the source. At times, the executive signature on the performance source code is very small, yet small deviations to a performance source code can devastate significant parts of the business. Here is a not so subtle example:

Do you know how when two strategic business functions need to work together to be successful, yet they cannot seem to get it going in a constructive and respectful way? One side is always blaming the other side and the result is that performance is poor, the customer stands to get something later or worse than expected and the struggle continues. Often these poor performing collaborations exist for months, in some cases for years. It is a major block to customer satisfaction, innovation and an efficient process strategy.

Understanding performance sources codes cuts through all this. When two functions are not working well, go directly to the source of this collaboration. How do the senior executives, responsible for each of these functions get along? What is the quality of their collaboration? What I often hear is, "They can't stand to be in the same room together." This is the problem. The dysfunctional relationship between two executives becomes the source code for the dysfunctional collaborative behavior between the two business functions. No amount of process optimization, lean management practices will significantly affect this situation. It is a waste of time and resource burn. The two executives involved must understand that they are responsible for the situation and these two either change their relationship, thus resetting the business collaboration or the executives need to be changed.

Executives, who—using language like the field of consequences, performance half-life and performance source codes in their leadership team conversations—understand quickly that this helps them look at their behavior, and the consequences, from a strategic perspective. While initially uncomfortable for some, teams that strive to play at their best recognize that this is valuable and beneficial terminology for their leadership team and their organization.

In Chap. 2, we will look at how dilemmas, dramas and differences affect an executive team's ability to play at their best.

References

1. Zeiler, J. (2017, July 20). *Trump's astounding interview—The blamer in chief.*. United States. CNN Online Publication. https://edition.cnn.com/2017/07/20/opinions/trump-astounding-interview-blamer-in-chief-opinion-zelizer/index.html.
2. Goldsmith, M., & Silvester, S. (2016). *Stakeholder Centered Coaching, maximizing your impact as a coach*. United States: THiNKaha Publishing Group.

2 Dilemmas, Dramas and Differences

Rarely addressed directly in the executive team, dilemmas, dramas and differences lie just below the water, ready to capsize the unsuspecting leader's ship.

2.1 Delicate Dilemmas

It is easy for a leadership team to become overwhelmed by the number and significance of the business issues that come at them on a daily basis. One result is that they do not take the time and space to clearly define and hold each other accountable for what it means to be a true member of the leadership team.

Before the Executive Ownershift process, it is not unusual to hear a senior leader respond like this:

"Do you want me to run my business function to the best of my abilities **or** do you want to me be a member of the executive team?"

You see the dilemma?

The answer is quite simply, yes. It is not a question of one OR the other, it is a matter of one AND the other. They go hand in hand, although this is easier said than done. I am not suggesting that this dilemma never surfaces after a team has committed themselves to Executive Ownershift. What I am saying is after addressing this in a meaningful way, teams become more adept at recognizing, managing and holding each other accountable to agreed standards in the team and this dilemma issue is not nearly as troublesome or time consuming. It no longer paralyzes or neutralizes a team's effectiveness, because team members know it must be managed; and what the costs are to the team and the organization if it is not.

If your company and senior leadership team roles do not take precedence over your functional and personal roles, your team will struggle to perform at its best. If leaders are always arguing about what to do from their own functional point of view and how it will impact their function, your executive team exchanges will resemble

D. Norenberg, *Executive Ownershift*, Management for Professionals,
https://doi.org/10.1007/978-3-030-35828-0_2

turf wars; in-fighting amongst team members for resources and talent leading to a toxic and low performance environment. This isn't an "all or nothing" switch, it's more of a give and take, but with that said, leadership teams that play at their best have their default setting at company interests and leadership team interests over function and personal interests.

There are five reasons leaders may favor their functional role over that of the executive team role:

(1) Most of their professional life is spent in a particular function and it has become a part of them. It is also where the majority, if not all, of their performance targets are, and how leaders are rewarded.
(2) There is no compelling overall executive team purpose that dissolves the dilemma leaders have with their specific function.
(3) The senior team collectively has not truly clarified what it does and what it doesn't do.
(4) Members do not experience the work in the senior leader team as important as their individual leadership functional work.
(5) Executive peers are not sure how to hold people accountable for team agreements and are even less sure if it is their job. (Many sit back and say, "That's what the CEO is here for.")

Sometimes the senior leader in an executive team is unsure how to resolve this dilemma. CEOs hold individual leaders responsible for their functional performance and how they operate their part of the business, yet rarely invest the time and energy to clarify and strengthen the leadership team identity; and the obligations and contributions that this requires.

For mediocre leadership teams, it is difficult to see this dilemma and to understand the negative impact this has on the organization. Tuned in CEOs listen carefully to how leader members talk about the leadership team dilemma. Some CEOs will act on it and others ask for advice to accelerate a constructive resolution to this dilemma in their team.

One way to approach this dilemma is by using an outside-in viewpoint. I speak with 12 to 18 leaders (not in the executive team) from their organization (selected by the CEO or even members of the leadership team) to get their perceptions of how they experience this group of people as a "leadership team". Here are some comments from different outside-in viewpoints before the dilemma was discussed and managed:

> What could this senior team improve? The messages that come out of the executive team are mixed up, meaning that different members have different understandings and interests. This isn't helpful and it is confusing.

> Some people in that team play political games well but are terrible managers. There seem to be no consequences for such behavior.

> Up to now, the executive team ran more like islands, people did their own thing and this was accepted behavior.

> At the executive level, the function heads don't seem to collaborate that well, R&D with sales, and sales with marketing as examples.

> In my view, these guys are all good leaders. We are missing the combined package; let us call this a real leadership team, speaking with one combined voice. Individually, they do well but it is not the same as one unit working together. The 1+1+1+1+1 formula does not add up yet for this team. Maybe you can help them become really one unit. The benefit would be very large for our organization and be motivating for all people.

The people I interview are direct reports to someone in the executive team. You can imagine how these perceptions cascade out through the rest of the organization and impact engagement and collaboration. A point to remember regarding dilemmas: they have significant consequences far beyond the leadership team.

When presented with these perceptions from people that report to them, it opens up the space for discussions on how to manage the functional and leadership team dilemma more effectively.

Benchmarks can be set to help "manage the dilemma" over time. Some helpful questions [1] for the leadership team include:

(1) How well and how often do we put issues on the table that may have negative implications for one's own function, even though it could be good for the overall business?
(2) To what degree do we keep leadership team discussions confidential until agreed upon that the content and results can be shared with the rest of the organization?
(3) What does our decision-implementation scorecard look like—do we carry through on decisions agreed upon by the team?
(4) Do we have standards in place and hold each other accountable for agreed upon behaviors that are consistent with our team standards?

Bill Russell, the American basketball icon, who won 18 basketball championships in his 21 years of playing (including 11 NBA championships in 13 years) said this, "Winning is the ultimate form of athletic expression. To win regularly, I learned to subordinate my individual goals so my team would be able to win. As a result, I become the kind of leader who understood that doing the most for my team would best guarantee success" [2].

2.2 Recurring Dramas

Charles, the technology CEO, was truly distraught. As he sat across the table from me, we exchanged our experiences about his recent executive off-site and Charles could not hide his frustration. He was involved in an ongoing tug-of-war with his Chief Marketing Officer and things just were not moving forward, for their relationship or the business.

From Charles's point of view, Eric, the CMO, had grown comfortable and complacent over the many years of running Marketing. Eric was not challenging himself or his marketing organization to innovate, in part because he and many in his group did not see the need to change and were not up to the future initiatives that Charles was aiming for. Over the past several months, Eric had circled the wagons around his people. His marketing strategy became defensive and he had his staff defend the status quo.

Charles and I had discussed Eric and this situation before, in fact many times. It had become his recurring drama. It was hurting the team and the business.

I had observed Eric in a number of settings and I could certainly appreciate the views that Charles shared. The two of them had discussed the topic numerous times and I had mediated a few of their exchanges without a real progress or change.

It was time to confront Charles with his recurring drama.

"Charles," I said, "this is a road you have been down many times before and you keep circling around it, consistently expressing your frustration, yet not getting results that satisfy you or the business."

"Dan, you know what the problem is; Eric has been here longer than the dinosaurs and if I ever tried to move him out of here, it would cost me an arm and a leg. In fact, due to our legacy compensation system, he makes nearly as much as I do, and I am the CEO!"

"Charles, if Eric wasn't in the picture here, how much more effective would your leadership team be and what would this mean for the business?" I inquired.

"We'd be at least 10% more effective, faster at our marketing initiatives and our growth rate would follow along those lines as well," he shot back.

"What was your revenue last year?" I asked.

"Just under 3.5 billion."

"So let me get this straight", I summarized, "you're saying that if you could make the change at the CMO level that this would impact and improve your business by 10%?"

"That's right."

"Charles, I studied psychology, not accounting, but even I can calculate what you believe this change would mean for your business. 10% of 3.5 billion is 350 million. What would it cost you to make the changes with Eric that you've thought about?"

"Probably 1.5 to 1.7 million."

"Let me understand this Charles," I said slowly, "You see an opportunity to make a change, create an upside for your business of 350 million against an 'investment' with Eric's departure of 1.5 million, right? What else is missing or needed for you to move forward, and not continue to circle around this drama that has clearly been consuming your time and energy?"

Eric was asked to leave a week later; respectfully and with a severance package that was agreeable to all parties. Additional changes were made in Eric's group that led to a more innovative, responsive, and client centered marketing approach and Charles's reoccurring drama was resolved. This gave a big boost to the entire executive team that had also been negatively affected by this recurring drama.

I share this story because on the surface, it looked like an easy decision for Charles. Yet simple as it sounds, Charles had not been able to look beyond his drama cycle and concretely develop alternatives, what ifs or explore the consequences of not resolving this drama.

Everyone can relate to such a situation. Playing at your best, as a leadership team, does not mean you avoid such dramas; but it means that you are highly aware of the importance of resolving recurring dramas that continuously cycle through team discussions.

When leadership teams do not recognize and deal with their recurring dramas, they pay for it three ways [3]:

(1) **Tangible Costs**—these are measurable losses, time, resources and people that are consumed or lost directly, because of the drama.
(2) **Intangible Costs**—these are softer costs, sometimes emotional in nature. The attitudes, energy and team spirit can sink very low when dilemmas are left hanging, infecting the team and the organization.
(3) **Peripheral Costs**—These are unexpected costs that are not considered when you start looking at a dilemma and its impact. In the case with Charles and Eric, two of the stronger talents in the Marketing group later shared with me that both of them had been seriously contemplating to leave the company, because of the Charles-Eric drama. This would have been a costly loss of talent for the company. Because of Charles's decision, they remained with the company, avoiding recruiting and on-boarding costs of new talent acquisition.

The closure of this drama brought renewed energy and momentum to the executive team and the marketing group created wins that confirmed the value of Charles's decision.

Executive Ownershift calls upon leadership teams to keep a watchful eye for recurring dramas in their team, between team members and in the organization that prevent them from playing at their best. Here are five ways to deal with disruptive dramas:

Name it and find out who owns it After a de-energizing, never-ending drama surfaces a few times, bring it into the team space. Giving the drama a provocative name makes it visible, more concrete and easier to deal with. Determining ownership helps set a timetable, process and plan together for resolution. Most dramas are not that difficult to dissolve, especially when outside expertise is called in to help.

Insist on three options There are alternatives and options to every drama and they help look beyond the story that is currently playing. While your final decision may be beyond the initial three options, it is a positive kick-starter to the process.

Visualize risks and rewards Breakthroughs come quickly when leaders visualize or map their dramas. Picturing the drama gives people the ability to see the issues with an external eye.

Lessons learned, looking back When stuck in the drama, ask yourself, 12 months from now, after I've resolved this drama, what are the benefits that our team and our business is experiencing and what lessons have I learned from the way I dealt with it? This brings a great opening into the space to deal with your drama.

Take another seat and get another view Had this discussion not been helpful for Charles, I could have asked him to take a different seat, meaning getting a different view on this recurring drama. This could have been views from Eric, other leadership team members, other people in the organization or customer viewpoints.

2.3 Turbo Charged Culture Clash

Simply because a group of men and women call themselves the executive leadership team, it does not mean that they automatically work together as an effective team. Leaders should not confuse arriving in the team with succeeding as a team. There is a big difference. Only after you arrive does the real work begin.

Leadership teams that ask me to support them often suffer from relationship deficiencies, meaning that leaders tend to see their executive peers primarily through the function they represent. Leadership teams that do not invest the energy and develop multi-dimensional or resilient relationships with each other fail to create the trusted space in their team that leads to:

- Honest conversations about their personal vulnerabilities or their real business challenges.
- Generous give and take between functions that serve the overall business first, then the functions.
- Resourcing each other for both their own leadership growth and cross-functional strategic success.

Through my experiences advising and coaching leadership teams, small differences between executives (when not managed properly) lead to big misunderstandings that cascade throughout the organization. Ironically, when leaders have the confidence and competence to address these differences early on, mutual understanding and agreements can be reached that transform differences into aligned action.

Addressing differences requires courage and the ability to stay in the conversation, even when things get warm and conflicted. Here is an example of how the sparks of conflict led to resilient relationships in one leadership team.

Missed milestones, cost overruns, and engines that were not suitable for flight summarize the situation I will share with you. I had been asked to step in and help moderate differences between members of a leadership team who were building high precision jet turbines for the aeronautics industry.

In addition to the missed business targets, the overall atmosphere and the willingness to work together had nearly come to a standstill. Had I been called in early, perhaps things would not have escalated as they had, nevertheless this was the situation and it needed to be dealt with.

The leadership team was very engineering driven and multi-cultural, and the strongest cultural dynamic was between the British and the German leaders. They had been butting heads for weeks and this leadership off-site was the beginning of a realignment process I had been asked to facilitate.

It was not long after the names, niceties and the priorities for the session were introduced that the team found itself facing off; in the British–German dynamic I mentioned earlier.

In this tense atmosphere, Rodger, the senior lead for the British team said, "I am just so tired of this play safe planning; the risk averse approach you Germans bring to this team is disrupting everything. At this pace, we will never finish on time or budget!"

One of the Germans stepped in to defend their planning practices, and Rodger, now exasperated, interrupted and jumped in again. He said, "You Germans are so obedient, so obsessed with following the rules that you would stand at the street corner, in the middle of the night, in the pouring rain waiting for the pedestrian red man signal to change to green."

Rodger was so angry that you could see the veins bulging in neck. "And if the light were broken, you'd stand in the rain all night long!"

On one hand, I was relieved that we'd come to the point of candid and emotional expression in the team, however I wasn't sure if or when I should intervene when Helmut, one of the Germans, whose English wasn't the best, leaned forward.

After pausing for a moment, Helmut said, "That's just the point, Rodger. In Germany, the light is never broken."

Helmut's direct comeback, hit Rodger (figuratively) right smack in the face. Rodger broke out in a smile and said, "Helmut, you are absolutely right, and that's the funniest thing I have heard you or anyone else in this team say in the past three months."

This story happened exactly as I have shared it with you and believe it or not, that exchange became a tipping point in this team's emotional dynamic. They were able to build a team that returned to established and agreed upon timelines, quality and cost milestones. Their success was part of a process that started when they began sharing their true perceptions of how they really experienced each other, especially when everyone was under such pressure. I observed that they began to listen to each other, and while doing so, gained an understanding that what one sees may have different meaning to someone from another culture.

One of the team exchanges that helped trigger the perception exchange I call, "A Basket of Surprises" and it works like this.

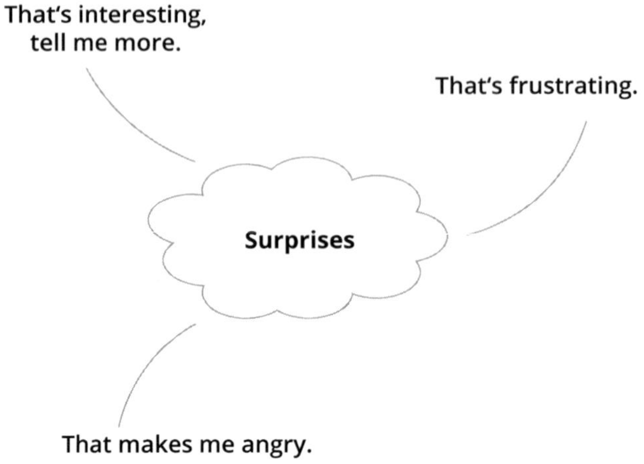

Fig. 2.1 Basket of surprises

On a flip chart, the team saw Fig. 2.1.

This visual became the prompt for a discussion about what aspects of another culture people found interesting, frustrating and what aspects of another culture made them angry? After the tension and air had been let out of the balloon through the Rodger-Helmut exchange, this discussion confirmed and dispelled beliefs they had about one another and through this honest exchange, they developed a better understanding for each other. This was the start of an ongoing process that took several months, sometimes with steps forward and sometimes with steps back. This give and take, with no winners or losers helped team members develop resilient relationships that eventually helped the team form a team identity that they felt was theirs.

This was an example that led to a breakthrough for this team. Although it looks simple now, looking back, it was not easy. It is not easy for business executives to express themselves at the risk of losing face, criticizing a colleague or simply saying how something makes them feel. Yet the courage to express how you experience small differences, and the ability to listen without judgement or a need to be right or win will open the door to a larger understanding, give trust some oxygen and support resilient relationship building.

2.4 House Rules for High Stakes Poker and Teams

Dilemmas, dramas and differences can derail the performance of any team. Do not make the mistake of trying to ignore or avoid them. The point is that all teams that struggle to play at their best will encounter one or more of these themes.

High performing leadership teams outpace mediocre teams by their ability to constructively address and manage these issues effectively.

How can you get busy and ambitious executives to slow down and consider the consequences of dilemmas, dramas and differences in their team and in their business?

You invite them to a game of high stakes poker.

Well, sort of. It is a card game, developed by Sivasailam Thiagaraja, called Barnga [4] and it resembles a poker tournament. Imagine you have an executive team of 12 people. I will set up four tables with three people at a table. Instructions are given and the aim of the game is to play the hand that you are dealt to "win" the hand with the best card.

Everything goes well until people change tables (like in any competitive tournament) and they encounter confusion, surprise, frustration and anger. They continue to play and move tables and people have varying degrees of success.

I should mention that during the game people are not allowed to speak.

We close the card game with a debriefing that helps people learn from their experience; here is what they often say:

> I moved to another table and they were cheating.

> They weren't as smart at the other table because they didn't understand the rules.

> I felt bad because at the start of the game I was winning, when I moved tables I wasn't successful anymore.

After they have shared their initial impressions, I ask them about the rules and if everyone had understood the rules before we started.

We thought so, they said.

Then I share that while I passed out a tournament guideline sheet and the rules at each table (which I picked up after their practice rounds), while similar, had some small differences, depending on which table they sat at.

This leads to a heated discussion and I asked what the tables and the cards could have represented for their business or their team.

"It could be different countries or cultures in our business or different functions or personalities in our team," they say.

The purpose of this poker game is to help leaders realize that while they may all be a part of the same leadership team, it does not automatically mean they play by the same rules. How people communicate, collaborate, make decisions and resolve conflict has a lot to do with their personality, the culture they come from and their professional experiences to date.

We simply cannot assume that because people wear the same company uniform that they understand the preferences and differences of their colleagues. This is why the Executive Ownershift process helps leadership teams define common guidelines that they can live by and thrive by.

Without having a common understanding, people can draw different conclusions from the same experience. It reminds me of a story an executive from Texas once shared with me.

A travelling preacher was making his way through the Bible belt, looking for folks that might want to attend his upcoming Christian revival sermon. He was driving through the countryside and he saw a farmer on the ground working under his tractor. The preacher parked his car and headed over to talk with him.

"I say good man, are you a member of the Christian family?" the preacher asks.

The farmer looked up from underneath the tractor and said, "Sir, the Christian family lives about two miles down the road."

The farmer did not catch the essence of the preacher message so he tried again. "No, no brother, I mean are you lost?"

The farmer is puzzled and replied, "No, I don't think so, I've been at this same farm for 30 years."

The preacher continues, "Brother, what I mean to ask you is, are you ready for the judgement day?"

The farmer pauses a moment and then asks, "Well, when is this judgement day?"

The preacher, exasperated says, "Well, I don't really know; it could be today or it could be tomorrow, it could be any day for that matter!"

The farmer pulls himself out from under the tractor, looks at the preacher, and says, "When you know when this judgement day is coming, please let me know as I think my wife would like to go both days."

Even if you have never been to Texas, the Bible belt or met a travelling preacher, you can still see how two people, who even speak the same language, take different meanings from this situation. It is not hard to understand how dilemmas, dramas and differences can derail a team from playing at its true potential.

It does not take a genius to see what makes people different, but it does take wisdom and patience to see what different people have in common [5].

References

1. Wageman, R., Nunes, D. A., Burrus, J. A., & Hackmann, R. J. (2008). *Senior leadership teams, what it takes to make them great*. Boston, MA: Harvard Business School Publishing Corporation.
2. Russell, B., & Falkner, D. (2001). *Russell rules, 11 lessons on leadership from the twentieth century's greatest winner*. New York: Penguin Group Publishing.
3. Weiss, A. (2008). *Value-based fees, how to charge and get what you are worth*. San Francisco, CA: Pfeiffer Publishing.
4. Thiagaraja, S., & Thiagaraja, R. (2006). *Barnga, a simulation on culture clashes*. London, UK: Nicholas Brealey Publishing.
5. Jones, L. B. (1997). *Jesus in Blue Jeans: a practical guide to everyday spirituality*. Santa Clara, CA: Hyperion.

Fractional Leadership 3

We live but a fraction of our lives.
—Henry David Thoreau

3.1 Fractions Do Not Lead to a Winning Formula

In chapters one and two, we looked at unique challenges facing senior leadership teams and the implications when executive teams do not manage these challenges effectively.

Lack of vulnerability, a do-not-start-here mentality, consequences of pretty-good leadership, dilemmas, dramas and cultural clashes are but a few of the executive challenges that prevent leadership teams and their organizations from playing at their best.

Old school and hero leadership advocates believe that the above challenges are characteristics common to "toughing it out at the top". Leaders with this mindset see the executive level as a battlefield, where competition, politics and power are played, often very subtlety and behind the scenes.

In other words, try harder.

I see it differently. Observing leaders that ignore or are unable to address the above-mentioned challenges constructively reminds me of a fly trying to get out of a room on a warm summer day. The fly, looking to escape the heat, continues to throw itself against the window, until it finally exhausts itself or dies. Ironically, if the fly would only make a slight adjustment, and stop trying so hard and simply try something different, it could find the open window only a few feet away.

We can all relate to the fly throwing itself against the window. We have been conditioned that when we want something, or things get difficult, all that is needed is to try harder.

Yet trying harder reinforces our already existing assumptions and does not lead to any breakthrough thinking or acting.

D. Norenberg, *Executive Ownershift*, Management for Professionals,
https://doi.org/10.1007/978-3-030-35828-0_3

What does trying harder look like in an executive meeting? Here is what one senior leader shared with me:

> Our executive meeting is more like a rooster meeting, everyone is really trying to show their best – you wouldn't dare show a weakness in this meeting.

You do not need to be a rocket scientist to understand what the operating assumptions in this leadership team are (refer back to Chap. 1 and the importance of vulnerability).

Yet the conditions described in chapters one and two often influence leaders to expose only a part of themselves, only a part of what is happening in their business, and little about what is working and not working with other executives in the leadership team. Lack of trust contributes to partial authenticity and people work hard to stay within parameters that they think are acceptable and safe.

This leads to fractional leadership; it is what happens when leaders do not create or engage with an open and holistic executive agenda. Fractional leadership means leaders only play a partial agenda, (usually theirs) and do not get help or feedback when they are not performing to the standards of excellence set by the entire team. Fractional leadership practices negatively influence the leadership team, which lead to:

- low employee engagement
- little willingness to challenge the status quo
- a lackluster strategy that does not create an intellectually clear and emotionally compelling story of their strategic future.

Thoreau's quote, "We live but a fraction of our life", supports my observations and experiences that the majority of executive teams lead with only a fraction of their leadership capability. Potential that could be transformed into performance. When this potential is not converted into performance at the executive level, how can anyone expect this to happen in other parts of the organization?

I ask members of an executive team how they would rate their leadership practice, if the number 1 signifies playing at their best. What fraction would they give themselves, as to how well they see their own performance? Executives share something like this:

$$3/4 + 5/6 + 7/8 + 1/2 + 2/3 + 2/3 + 3/3 + 5/8 = 17/3 \text{ or } 5.67 \text{ out of } 8$$

Think about the implications of this exercise. Eight members in the leadership team, yet in this example, they do not see themselves creating any synergistic value, which would be a value higher than the sum of individual members, something above eight. What is even more interesting, from my experience and reinforced by other experts is that up to 80% of executives surveyed believed they had the necessary skills to fulfill their role, but only 30% believed that all of their colleagues did [1].

In other words, a large number of executives rate themselves as able and capable, but not many of their team members. At what point does an executive reach across the aisle and offer help? Probably never if I do not feel safe and secure to share my challenges, or concerned about the blow back I will get if I share my views with another executive.

Perfection is not the point. None of us is perfect and to date I have never met a leader that does not have some area in which they can improve, and of course, this goes for leadership teams too.

Yet when leadership teams accept that they contribute heavily to the source code of their organization's performance, they see how their behaviors and operating patterns lead to "poor performance code". They recognize that poor source code creates less than optimal results in their organization. They begin to own their fractional leadership practices and this means they can begin the shift to writing new code, and the road to better leadership practices and improved organizational results.

You might ask, if the executive team is comprised of the best and the brightest people in the company, how and why do these fractional leadership practices get started in the first place?

Just because you have a selected group of highly intelligent, experienced and ambitious leaders as the executive leadership team, this does not automatically mean they will come together as a highly effective leadership team.

3.2 Ten Obstacles to High Performance

In addition to the challenges mentioned in chapters one and two, there are ten obstacles (that consistently come to the forefront in my years of working with executives)—that sideline leadership teams from playing at their best. While not complicated or difficult to understand intellectually, the ability to address and overcome these obstacles requires awareness, action and follow through from all leadership team members.

1. **Dutifully Distracted**

Does your leadership team resemble a firefighting unit? Is your leadership team reacting instead of actively driving strategic initiatives?

Senior leadership teams are confronted with a multitude of problems and opportunities to address, many of them distractions that should not rise to the senior team in the first place. Everyone wants something from the company's senior executives and this is where most teams make the mistake of jumping into their company's business issues too deeply at the beginning of their team's evolution. This fast start often means a fractional start, because leadership teams do not spend enough time, nor create the right structures for their team to perform at their best. Once they surround themselves with company issues, they have little time, patience or energy to address their fractional leadership practices.

2. **Power Over Trust**

In leadership teams, there is a lot at stake. There is a great deal of power and often not much trust. A senior leader is rarely going to tell their colleagues, "I'm not sure how to handle this situation." If someone does say, "I have a problem," they do it in a confessional way with a coach, so no one else knows about it.

3. **Executive Isolation**

There is a layer of insulation that prevents senior leaders from hearing the truth about how others perceive them and the real state of the business. Too often leaders get good news that keeps them happy, yet distracted from the issues that could help their business really shine. Signs of executive isolation sound like this:

> I'd like to see more constructive conflict in our organization.
>
> Why didn't we hear about this resource problem earlier?
>
> Nobody gives me pushback.
>
> How on earth could we miss our sales forecast by so much?

It would be easy to look at an executive team's direct reports and assume that they are not aware of the situation or are reluctant to share the good, the bad and the ugly with their superiors. In my experience, it is the latter. When executive leaders feel left out of the information loop or get information just before the train is going to hit the wall, it is often the result of unintentional patterns by executives themselves that lead to the isolation syndrome. In most cases, they are not even aware that their own actions lead to this condition. If you and members of your executive team feel isolated, there is a good chance that it is self-inflicted.

4. **Feedback Vacuum**

Nothing grows in a vacuum. The lack of oxygen in a vacuum environment prevents this. It is no different in leadership teams. When you have a feedback vacuum, meaning executive leaders do not give feedback to each other about behavioral or business issues, those things they do well and where they fall short, leaders, nor their business, will grow.

I interviewed members of an executive team who were struggling to regain their business competitiveness. During my perception gathering sessions with them, one by one they shared the following:

> We are not used to give feedback to each other. We've somehow lost this and we would like to learn how to do this as part of a normal activity.
>
> We get lazy very easily – we need to build a real culture of thoughtful feedback amongst ourselves.
>
> We don't benefit from the experience of the others – this is a pity as there are smart guys in the room.

5. **Learning Slower than the Real Rate of Change**

How fast is your business moving? If you are a senior leader in a competitive company, I am going to guess that things are moving fast in your business, especially today. Do the comments sound familiar to you?

> We need to recognize that this isn't the good old days any more. We must change the way we think and do things.

> Our growth rates are declining and our margins are shrinking – we are not used to this change.

If you always do what you have always done, you will always get what you always got. Fractional leadership practices often occur simply because leadership behavior and performance, which was appropriate and successful at one point in time, is no longer competitive. High performance leadership teams recognize this and are constantly challenging themselves to "up their game" so they are learning faster than the rate of change in their business. Dr. Marshall Goldsmith addresses this theme well in his bestseller, "What Got You Here, Won't Get You There." [2].

Take Jesse Owens, multiple gold medal winner in the 1936 Olympics. At the time Owens won his four gold medals, he was the fastest human on the planet. Now, just less than 100 years later, Owen's gold medal winning time in the 100-yard dash would not even be fast enough to win in the qualifying round heats. We must retain our core skills and adapt or change those things that no longer help us lead competitively.

6. **Waiting for the Next New Thing**

Information overload is not reserved exclusively for today's youth, who are exposed to more information in one month than their grandparents were over a lifetime [3]. Executive and strategic leaders are bombarded with theories, styles, diagnostics and principles to support their efforts. Well-meaning advisors, coaches and business schools all proclaim to have the next sure fix for leadership ailments. Yet with all these resources at their fingertips, is the quality and performance of leadership today better than it was, say 100 years ago?

This subject brings debates and lively discussions to any leadership team dinner. Like trying to compare apples and oranges, leading a complex global organization today is not the same as leading a business one hundred years ago. The breadth and diversity of global business, the speed and complexity of current technologies and the highly demanding client expectations make leading today a hugely challenging endeavor. Is more theory, style and principles the answer for today's leaders?

The challenge many leaders, and their leadership teams suffer from today is that they believe that the next new thing may be the cure for their executive challenges.

Experienced leadership developers have certainly heard the following, "Today was interesting, but actually I had heard most of what we talked about before." We should not confuse discussions around leadership tools with the next blockbuster movie, where something new or different is needed to sell more movie tickets. Leaders that say, well I did not hear anything new, are often the most reluctant to show what they can do, instead of what they know. Highly effective leadership is about doing the things that matter most, not just knowing them.

So in addition to starting with yourself, high performance leadership isn't always about starting something new; often it's about stopping or changing a fractional leadership pattern. As you move to higher and higher leadership levels in your company, you are less likely to get feedback about behaviors, habits or communication patterns that you practice, particularly negative ones, which means it's harder and harder (at the executive level) to spot and address fractional leadership issues. Dr. Peter Drucker said, "Half the leaders I have met don't need to learn what to do. They need to learn what to stop." [3]. Knowing and learning how to stop fractional leadership practices I would say.

7. **Unwilling to Own and Practice the Lincoln Law of Self Improvement**

In the introduction, I introduced the Lincoln Law of Self Improvement, which means never seeing oneself as a "finished product" or without any potential to convert into new growth practices. The surest way to succeed, from Lincoln's perspective was to improve himself, not expect others to change. Denying that learning and change begin at the executive level is a sure sign that nobody else will take ownership of it either.

8. **Failure to Instill Team Systems for Continuous Improvement**

When leaderships play at their best, we see that they have made explicit team rules and standards of excellence that hold team members accountable, often with an outside resource that serves as an advisor or team coach for them. It is very difficult, and in fact unfair, to ask Human Resources to provide the support needed at this level. Rarely does this department have the standing to challenge the senior leadership team, their capability or performance, as they report into these senior executive teams.

These standards of excellence are part of an overall system for continuous improvement for the leadership team, which easily cascades throughout the rest of the organization.

9. **Heady but not Hearty**

As stewards and guardians of the overall organization, it is tempting to see their role as money managers or simply guardians for the financial results of the business. While this is an important aspect of executive leadership, it distracts some leadership teams from creating strong emotional and intimate bonds with their leadership colleagues. Being hearty does not mean trying to be best friends with everyone in the leadership team, but it does mean striving and insisting on respectful, open and trust based relationships. We will look at this in more detail in Chap. 5.

10. **Uncertain Ownership**

Who owns the executive agenda? More importantly, to what degree have you and your senior leadership team colleagues clarified what your executive team agenda is? If there is uncertainty related to your executive agenda, it is impossible to have unified joint ownership of this agenda at the senior level.

In fact, when I asked leadership teams what their executive agenda is, I get different responses.

Some think the executive agenda is the organization's strategic plan.

Others think that it is a series of events in the life of an executive.

Still others think it is the actual agenda at an executive meeting.

The executive agenda is not a plan. It is the collective output of your leadership team.

The executive agenda is like a film of how relevant others perceive, experience and are influenced by the senior leadership team. Relevant others include stakeholders, shareholders, colleagues, peers, staff and customers. If you feel that parts of your organization do not show the ownership you expect of them, come back to the clarity, alignment and ownership of your executive agenda.

Over the course of the last three chapters, we have looked at what prevents bright, ambitious and business savvy leaders from operating as a high performance leadership team. Yet for those teams that master the challenges we have looked at, the rewards are significant.

3.3 It Is Not About Trying Harder

Even in executive teams, brimming with natural talent, huge amounts of intellectual firepower and ambition, this alone is not enough to create a highly effective leadership team.

We have to be honest with ourselves. The playing field that leaders perform on has changed dramatically in the past 30 years. With more and more executive coaches, business schools, and consultancies promising results with new leadership models, interventions and diagnostic instruments, we must face the fact that we are failing to create and support highly innovative and effective leadership teams. Leadership teams are the growth engines for your organizations. Simply start in your own organization—how many of your executive and senior leadership teams are playing at their best?

It is not about trying harder. It is about doing things differently.

It means an executive ownershift.

References

1. Herb, E., Leslie, K., & Price, C. (2001, May). Teamwork at the top. *McKinsey Quarterly*. United States. McKinsey Group.
2. Goldsmith, M., & Reiter, M. (2008). *What got you here won't get you there. How successful people become even more successful*. United States: Profile Books.
3. Drucker, P. F. (2001). *The essential Drucker, the best of sixty years of Peter Drucker's essential writings on management*. United States: Collins Business Essentials.

Executive Ownershift 4

Executive Ownershift, two words that will change the course of your leadership team and your company.

4.1 The Tipping Point

I am convinced that if you really want to get ahead of your competition and stay ahead as a market leader, the place you have to start at is at the top with the leadership team. Anything else is a distraction. This chapter is about how I learned that change, improvement and growth starts at the top.

It was the end of October and time for the 60-day follow through review session with Kevin. He was the president of a $500 million technology company and this review session was the last part of the strategic execution project with his executive team and the next two leadership levels in his organization. In total, about 80 people participated and I was eager to hear how the work from the final strategic off-site was taking hold in their organization.

The meeting was going pretty well, Kevin seemed happy with the results as he updated me on the progress over the past 60 days. On the surface, everything seemed fine, but I could not help but feel there was something under the surface that Kevin was not sharing with me.

I stepped in, "Kevin, this is fine and good; I'm happy that you and the executive team are pleased with the work we did together, but to be honest, it feels like there's something on your mind that you're not sharing with me."

Kevin was quiet. After a while he said, "We are happy with the results, we identified our strategic issues and over the course of the off-site we developed a good plan of execution and follow through."

"So what's the issue," I asked.

D. Norenberg, *Executive Ownershift*, Management for Professionals,
https://doi.org/10.1007/978-3-030-35828-0_4

Kevin began slowly, "Well, if I am really honest with you, although this strategic process was good and we felt the final strategic off-site was very powerful; now looking at what has actually happened, I would have expected more things to have changed faster in our business, since this off-site."

"Now we were coming to the core issues," I thought to myself.

I thanked Kevin for his honesty and then begin to probe what changes he had made in his personal leadership approach, changes in the way he was spending his time now, as opposed to before our strategic off-sites. I also asked what changes the executive team had followed through on and how did the next level perceive these changes.

It became an uncomfortable moment and Kevin realized neither he, nor his team, had truly committed and followed through at their level. Instead, they were watching and waiting for the project workhorses to carry forward on the project agreements reached during the off-site.

Yet these project agreements were also tied to agreements by members of the executive team, individually and collectively. Little had moved at the very top and as uncomfortable as that moment was, Kevin realized that the change he was expecting in others should have started with him and his leadership team.

4.2 Early Days of Executive Ownershift®

The October conversation with Kevin was not just a tipping point for him. It was also a tipping point for me personally. It helped me realize that there was a bigger issue at play than the work that I had been doing, so let me provide some context.

As managing director and senior partner of our consultancy practice at this time, my team and I provided consulting and development projects in leadership, change management, team building and intercultural competencies for companies like the Allianz Group, Biotronik, Ciba Vision, DentsplySirona, the European Patent Office, Klosterfrau, Knorr-Bremse, Rohde & Schwarz, and ZF TRW, to name a few.

Our work focused on first time leaders up through strategic leaders, usually stopping one or two levels below the executive team. We did good work, clients were happy with our results and over the course of twenty years; we successfully designed and led programs for 20,000 professionals (73 nationalities) in 26 countries on three continents.

The vice president of HR or the CEO's office would approach me from time to time and ask if I would be interested in helping the executive team with "some of their issues." Eager for new challenges and pleased to see that our work was interesting and attractive to other areas of their business, I accepted the invitations to help.

After the initial niceties, and pre-briefings, I often heard, "Don't expect too much to come from working with this group, you're the third consultant they have worked with already this year, so we hope you understand we can't make any significant commitments to you that this will go on".

"Fine with me, let's see how things go," I said.

This was the setting, some 15 years ago, that gave birth to Executive Ownershift®. Over the past fifteen years, as more requests from the top came in, more and more of my time has been spent advising, consulting and coaching executive and senior leadership teams. Now, after working hands-on with more than 100 leadership teams, I felt it was time to consolidate these experiences and share what must go right and what can go wrong for leadership teams that cannot afford to play at less than their best.

This calling to work with leadership teams was more than a job, it felt like my personal mission and something I was born to do. While I had seen a multitude of leadership initiatives over the years, all started with the best of intentions, nearly all of them were overlooking the importance of helping leadership teams, as an organizational and learning unit, to play at their best.

"How can change, improvement and growth start anywhere else except the top?" I asked myself.

This personal mission became so important to me that I was prepared to leave behind the successful learning consultancy that I had built over the previous 20 years in order to focus on this new calling.

My new mission would be to serve and support leadership teams to truly exploit their individual and collective leadership potential, using all of the know-how and show-how I had gathered from my years of experience. "When leadership teams truly set the example they expect of others, and in effect *reown their executive agenda*, this vivid example will cascade through the organization," I reasoned.

I was convinced that while each leadership team is special and unique; there are distinctions and patterns of success that separate leadership teams that are just getting by, from those that thrive and succeed through continually adapting to their changing business environment.

Leadership team success never appears in isolation. In other words, when your executive team performs well, so do people in your organization. I had never encountered a high performance organization run by a failing leadership team. Conversely, I had not experienced a highly effective leadership team that sat on top a lackluster organization. Their mutual success, or failure, went hand in hand.

4.3 My Beliefs for Executive Ownershift

I believe that leadership teams are everything to the success of your business. This is core to my work and fundamental to my client's success. My work with leadership teams is based on the belief that people have the right to lead at their very best and those who follow deserve to be led by those who are playing at their best. This means to me the pragmatic pursuit of purpose and success, not the paralyzing process of trying to be perfect.

This starts with the senior leadership team.

Most organizations and mainstream consultants see leadership as an individual endeavor. This is not the most effective approach because your company's success depends on the effective teamwork and collaboration of your leaders, not their individual talents. An executive team is often a collection of highly talented and experienced leaders, but not functioning as a highly effective team. Yet these leadership teams are the organic engines of growth and results in your organization and deserve the opportunity to develop and improve, as a team and not simply as a fragmented collection of individual leaders. In the language of Executive Ownershift, leadership is a team sport.

Management expert and master mentor, Dr. Alan Weiss says this about the team construct, and creating organizational results:

> There is no route I know that leads from individual contribution, no matter how excellent or innovative, directly to organizational goals. The catalyst that turns individual effort into organization results by the synergy of teamwork [1].

Far too often, people improvement and growth is addressed "bottom up", because senior leaders are too busy with other issues, think they are already good enough, or are reluctant to address their challenges publicly. This cannot be the example that leads to an organization performing at its best. If you want to change your business, leaders must change themselves. You can only improve and grow your business when leaders improve and grow. This should not start at the bottom of your organization; it should start at the top. From my experience, executives that have the courage and discipline to share that growth and improvement begin with them and then follow through create strong emotional bonds with people who are eager to follow such an example.

You can lead a horse to water, however you cannot make him drink. My mission and purpose is not about converting non-believers to Executive Ownershift; it is about attracting leaders who think and believe that leadership is a matter of example that begins and ends with them.

If you believe that breakthrough growth, dramatically increasing the speed of change and a culture of ownership in your organization can be created without the executive and senior leadership teams leading the way, well, that is your choice, and we can respectfully agree to disagree.

4.4 Executive Ownershift Cornerstones

The four cornerstones of high performance leadership teams, shown in Fig. 4.1, are anchored deeply into the transformational growth process called executive ownershift. High performance leaders focus on creating an emotional attachment between themselves, their employees and their business. They focus on culture before results, people before processes. This is not to say that results and processes

Fig. 4.1 Executive ownershift cornerstones

are not important, they are vital to the success of any business. Nevertheless, the approach, people and culture first, lies at the heart of Executive Ownershift. If you want to change your business, you have to change yourself. If you want to grow your business, you have to create team growth, which comes through people growth.

Inspiring others through best leadership team examples

Ralph Waldo Emerson said, "*What you do thunders above your head so loudly, I cannot hear the words you speak.*" Leaders that walk the talk together are truly an inspiring bunch to work for.

Leading a senseful strategy throughout your business

All too often, strategy becomes an intellectual exercise that ends up in somebody's desk drawer. You will learn how to create and lead a senseful strategy after you have completed Chap. 7.

Create the conditions for an ownership culture

Ownership, the highest form of engagement, cannot be assigned or delegated. We will look at the steps to create the conditions needed to have your invitations accepted for an ownership culture in Chap. 8.

Put the customer at the center of everything you do

There are many mantras that leaders use to excite and engage people across their organization—yet there is nothing as unifying and personally rewarding as having an entire organization aligned and unified to serve their customers above all. We will look at how you put the customer at the center of everything you do in Chap. 10.

4.5 The Significant Six

Executive Ownershift can be seen as a "cycle of shifts". Rational, emotional and behavioral shifts all coming out of the work initiated by senior leaders. This enables leadership teams to get to the core of their purpose and meaning for being, as an organizational unit. When you get your purpose right, it begins to argue for itself. We should not forget, leaders are mega-multipliers—this is why Executive Ownershift is an effective and worthwhile investment for leadership teams that aspire to play at their best.

"How do I know whether my executive team is practicing and promoting the principles of Executive Ownershift?" leaders ask me. The "SIGNIFICANT SIX" hits at the heart of high performance leadership teams, developed from my years of observation and experiences with high performance leadership teams.

Reflect on your personal experiences in your leadership team and use them to encourage an *"executive ownershift"* discussion in your next leadership meeting.

If you strongly agree with the statement, give yourself 15 points. If you somewhat agree, give yourself 10 points. If you somewhat disagree, give yourself 5 points and if you strongly disagree, do not give yourself any points for that statement. Your score will be somewhere between 90 and 0.

_______________ The leadership behaviors in our executive team excite and engage people in our organization.

_______________ Our executive team collaborates and supports each other in such a way that it sets the positive example for others in our company.

_______________ Our executive team leads the most effective meetings in our company.

_______________ Our business strategy is clear and emotionally compelling, due to the effort and example set by the executive team.

_______________ High performance and exceptional results in our business can be directly linked to the effectiveness of our executive team.

_______________ Our executive leadership team is playing at its best.

Significant six scorecard

Points scored	Leadership team considerations
90–80	Congratulations—You are a highly effective leadership team; let me invite you and your team to lunch
79–70	Pretty good, what is missing for you to perform at your best? (Remember the consequences of "pretty good" leadership from Chap. 1)
69–60	Bordering mediocre, if you are the company's best, where is everyone else?
59 and below	What is holding you back from making the changes you expect in others?

As this work continued to develop, I knew that leadership teams needed a language, framework and process so that they could take what they learned and quickly move this into their own organizations. Executive Ownershift, in my eyes, is serious play, and leaders who learned how it worked for them would later become teachers with conviction and passion, thus magnifying the results throughout their business.

While some of the language that I am sharing may be new to you (i.e. field of consequences, performance half-life, source codes, and fractional leadership); if you are a senior leader, you recognize the situations behind of the terminology I have used. This ability to come quickly to the real issues, address them in vivid language, and enable teams to reown their plan of action becomes the trademark of teams that play at their best.

The signature team strengths is not a linear process, rather it describes the touchstones of excellence consistent with high performance leadership teams. Here is a highlight for each signature strength (Fig. 4.2).

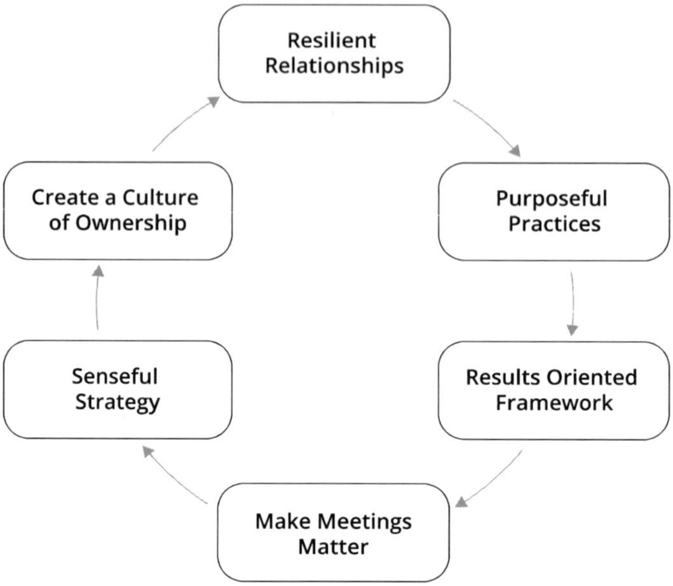

Fig. 4.2 Signature team strengths

Resilient Relationships

To what degree do relationships in your leadership team recover quickly from difficult situations and discussions? Is there an active and dynamic feedback process present amongst team members? Do sacred cows and white elephants get discussed openly and candidly? Resilient relationships are fundamental to a high performance leadership team, and you will find ideas and advice in Chaps. 2, 5, 8 and 9.

Purposeful Practices

What is the purpose of your leadership team? Can each member of the leadership team describe the unique contributions you offer to the organization and the marketplace? Has the leadership team identified its best practice charter or standards of excellence from which it operates and do members hold others accountable to these agreements?

Results Oriented Framework

Clear roles and responsibilities, an effective communication system, providing timely feedback and clear decision making processes lead to a results oriented framework [2].

Make Meetings Matter

There is too much cruising in senior leadership meetings. Not only do executives miss opportunities to accelerate the impact of their leadership decisions in the business, they set a "cruising culture" for everyone else in the organization. This costs your business huge amounts of money and gives competitors that make meetings matter an advantage over you that need not be. Refer to Chap. 6 to learn how to make your meeting the best in your company.

Leading a Senseful Strategy

A senseful strategy is purposeful, significant and full of sense, *enabling you and everyone else in the organization* to make choices and take decisions that support the nature and direction of your business. In Chap. 7, you will see how to ensure that your strategy is truly senseful.

Creating an Ownership Culture

Money might buy love, but you cannot buy an ownership culture for your organization. To create a culture of ownership in your business, insist that people have control over the outcomes they create. Help people throughout your organization see how the business is improving and be sure that folks who work in your company feel that their work is recognized and contributes to the overall growth of your business. In Chap. 8, I share how to create an ownership epidemic in your organization.

4.6 Beyond Business as Usual

Executive Ownershift is different than other social technologies, because unlike other initiatives, executive leaders cannot be bypassed, opt out or be too busy to personally involve themselves with Executive Ownership® because it starts with senior leadership teams.

There are many initiatives, (developing company values, management principles, performance management) where executive acceptance suffices. In Executive Ownershift, acceptance is no replacement for ownership. This means personal involvement, expression of vulnerability, willingness to fail and the courage and discipline to create and live by a culture of consequences. These conditions are the precursors to creating an ownership culture in your organization.

Executive Ownershift is real time learning with real time issues for real time results. It is more than an individual experience, it is a team of leaders' experience, learning, reflecting and adapting while you run your business. It runs along side your everyday business and serves you best when you and your business have a plateful of priorities to deal with. In other words, it is not a spectator sport and it requires leaders to become players, not passengers in the change and growth they expect in others.

This is the owner shift in the most personal sense.

Executive Ownershift cannot be reached from inside the comfort zone. As you read in the first three chapters, and perhaps from your personal experience, you know that some executives would prefer to hide their vulnerabilities than share them with their team and others. (Imagine the example this sets for the rest of the organization.) Yet when they do share, this release of honesty and authenticity within the team leads to deeper intimacy and higher levels of trust. This cannot be contained (thank goodness) and spreads organically throughout the organization and expanded thinking and acting begin to take hold.

4.7 Your Game Changer

Conversations like the one with Kevin at the beginning of this chapter are the tipping point for transformational change for a leadership team and their organization.

Regardless of industry or geographical location, use these "game changing questions" to help stretch yourself beyond running the everyday business:

- How would your leadership team operate if your organization improved every day?
- How would you and your leadership team need to change to create a culture that moves beyond responsibility and accountability to ownership, and thereby deep personal engagement?
- How do you enable everyone in your organization to put the customer at the center of everything they do?
- To accelerate innovation, strategic execution and growth across your organization, what needs to take place in your leadership team?
- Who are the key stakeholders in your executive agenda and how well does your leadership team meet and exceed their expectations?

After asking these questions, I listen carefully how executives answer them; and continue to reflect the questions back to the executive leaders, so that I can understand where they see the tipping point for change, and potentially the catalytic mechanism [3] that could trigger a new approach or direction for their business.

It is exciting and compelling when executives say, "Dan, this begins with us, it's about how we operate as a leadership team". Leaders like Dr. Lars Hendrikson at Dentsply Sirona, Markus Miederhoff at UBS, Jacques Richier at Allianz France and Dietrich Fechner at Ciba Vision all have pointed out, in their own words, that if they want to change their business, it starts at the top of their organization.

The executives mentioned above and hundreds of others I have worked with understand that leadership teams who want to play at their best have to get beyond day-to-day business. By asking these questions and looking for the links between what is happening (or not happening in the business) and how it connects to the work in the leadership team is one of the tipping points to profit from the Executive Ownershift process.

Although the ideas and solutions to these questions change over time, the fundamental need for leadership teams to "take ownership" and learn faster than the rate of change to develop solutions that customers find attractive and "value full" continues. Those that get it thrive, (Amazon) and those that do not (Sears) die.

Three situations where Executive Ownership can accelerate your leadership team growth and organizational results:

Quick Start

You are a senior leader who has recently taken over a new executive team or you are new to the organization and it is critical that you get off to a successful and fast start. When Markus Miederhoff, General Counsel and Group Head of Employment Legal at UBS asked me to work with him and his leadership team, he put it this way.

> Certainly I have a great deal of experience and a successful track record in my previous roles, yet there is much to navigate through in this new role, in a new organization, and with a brand new team. I see this process with you as "good insurance and a catalyst" to get our Global Legal Team off to a successful start.

Yesterday's Performance

Past success does not guarantee a winning future. It is challenging enough to win the title in a season; yet to duplicate that becomes more difficult. Executive Ownershift can help you and your leadership team in situations where you were highly successful in the past but now your performance has you fading back in the pack.

Dr. Lars Hendrikson, Global VP of Implants at DentsplySirona, asked me to work with him and his leadership team. The leadership team practices that were successful in the past no longer provided the impact to the organization, the customers and the business results that they had previously.

Lars and his team created a more meaningful and emotionally compelling business strategy that put the customer in the center of everything they do. This, along with a robust realignment of what the leadership team should do and should not do, as well as standards of excellence developed to build stronger and more authentic accountability guidelines in the team are helping them return to higher performance and growth. (More from Lars in Chap. 9.)

Once in a Lifetime or Disruptive Tsunami

"There are opportunities that come once in a lifetime", Jacques Richier, CEO of Allianz France shared with me after he was asked to guide an internal multi-billion dollar merger between three highly successful business lines that had little in common, according to many critics.

Jacques and a collection of senior executives from diverse businesses worked with the Executive Ownershift principles to successfully merge three Allianz businesses into one. Global Automotive, Allianz Assistance and Allianz Worldwide Care have successfully become Allianz Worldwide Partners (AWP) under CEO Richier.

Leaders that find themselves in the midst of an incredible opportunity that comes only once in a lifetime or are suffering from one of the most disruptive events in their business history can use the Executive Ownershift process as a stabilizing rudder and a strong set of sails at your back to create the deeply engaging ownershift that will guide your team and your business to success.

4.8 It Is Not a Matter of More Money

Senior executives and their HR teams pour huge amounts of money into people development but they are not getting a good return on their investment. According to Beer, Finnström and Schrader in "Why Leadership Training Fails – and What to Do About It" [4], American companies alone spend 350 billion dollars worldwide for learning, that for the most part, doesn't lead to better organizational performance, because people soon revert back to their own ways. Learning and development investments pay much higher dividends when the development initiative involves the entire leadership team. Only working with the intact leadership team can you ensure that you address both leadership and team development, as well as organizational improvements.

Complaints that leadership and personal development is not paying huge dividends is often because the initiatives are too individually focused, the learning sets are artificially constructed (teams create results not HR talent pools) or there is not enough real time business in the room with practice—in other words, too abstract or discussion driven.

Your business does not deliver value through talent pools. Value is created through technical teams, sales teams, cross-functional teams, and above all, leadership teams. It is high time that professionals practice and learn in the units where they work.

Think about it for a minute. Imagine an orchestra that didn't practice together, that didn't learn together, what do you think their performance would be like if they all practiced alone, without the dynamics, complications and the interactions of one another?

When you watch any first class team, regardless of the sport, profession or practice; you will see that they spend huge amounts of time, together, working on the fundamentals of their craft and in the situations where they need to perform as a team. High performance teams also take time to reflect on their past games or team experiences and look to learn and improve from those experiences.

You may be thinking to yourself, "What happened after Kevin's tipping point conversation on that October morning?"

As tough as that conversation was, Kevin "owned up" to his role in the strategic execution. It became a personal mission for him. Kevin asked me to stay involved, we conducted more reviews with the team and through some frank and revealing conversations, developed the commitments and ownership needed to show changes at the top of the business as well as within the key projects.

Less than two years after our tipping point conversation, Kevin's organization was acquired by a much larger organization that was seen as hugely beneficial to all parties, including the customers. There were generous compensation packages offered to all and it was a storybook ending.

"Dan, your Executive Ownershift process is common sense," executives tell me.

Common sense does not always translate into common practice. Common sense is about knowing, common practice is about doing. This is important to remember when we address titanic challenges in Chap. 5.

References

1. Weiss, A. (1994). *Best laid plans: Turning strategy into action throughout your organization.* United States: Macalester Park Pub Co.
2. Larson, C., & LaFasto, F. (1989). *Teamwork, what must go right, what can go wrong*. United States: Sage Publications.
3. Collins, J. (2001). *Good to great, why some companies make the leap—And others don't.* United States: Random House Business.
4. Beer, M., Finnström, M., & Schrader, D. (2016, October). *Why leadership training fails—And what to do about it.* United States: Harvard Business Review.

5 Mastering Titanic Challenges

What part of the iceberg really sunk the Titanic?

5.1 Shortly Before Midnight

As the RMS Titanic sped through the Atlantic on a moonless night, little concern was given to the pack ice and icebergs that filled the waters off Newfoundland. Not only was the luxury liner considered unsinkable, it was also a commonly held belief, even among experienced sea masters, that icebergs posed no real threat to state-of-the-art ships of the era.

Yet sink she did, and in the months, years and decades that followed, the Titanic has been the focus and scrutiny of public inquiries, government legislation, maritime regulations and even films. Today, over 100 years after the tragedy, the Titanic continues to capture the attention of scientists, seafarers, engineers, and the public at large.

There is much to learn from the Titanic experience. Whether through the lens of decision making, communication, moral leadership (passenger safety and exit strategies depended on what class you travelled in) or strategic execution; each viewpoint offers valuable lessons of how people performed (or did not) in this crisis.

Yet at the most fundamental level, let us remember that the Titanic, the most technological advanced luxury liner of its time, was fatally damaged on its starboard hull by part of an iceberg that was not even visible to the human eye. It sank and over 1,500 people died.

What does this mean for leadership teams today?

D. Norenberg, *Executive Ownershift*, Management for Professionals,
https://doi.org/10.1007/978-3-030-35828-0_5

5.2 Iceberg Realities

It is not the visible part of the iceberg that threatens most leadership teams; it is the larger part of the iceberg that is hidden from view, which represents titanic challenges.

Let me explain.

To play at their best, executive teams must manage two realities, represented by the iceberg, shown in Fig. 5.1.

The material reality: The visible part of the iceberg above the water; and

the non-material reality: The aspects that are not seen, not written about and seldom talked about.

Business leaders understand the **material reality**: sales forecasts, strategy, the balance sheet, product launches, and regulatory guidelines. This is the leader's reality that is above the water, it is observable, measurable and objective in nature. At the end of the month, or reporting period, you can look and determine whether you have been successful or not. The material reality can be evaluated and judged, because these are things based on an objective truth. You deliver on your business

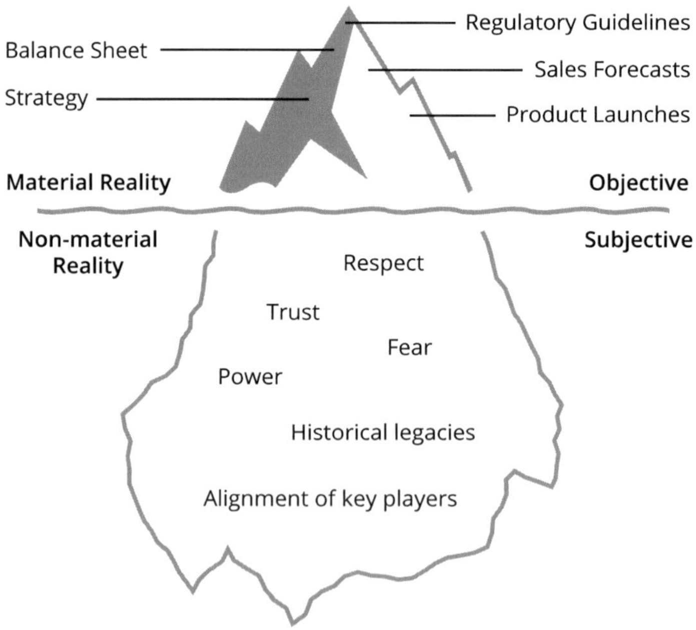

Fig. 5.1 Iceberg realities [1]

plan or not. The machines in the production run or they do not. This is the world of hard facts.

Hard facts are vital for business success; we are constantly reminded to "know your business", meaning have a good understanding of your numbers and how they contribute to your business success. Yet the leadership teams that I have worked with come to realize that success in the material reality comes about by effectively managing what is under the iceberg.

Non-material reality or themes include the degree of trust, respect, and openness that is practiced by team members. What is the collaboration quality between key players and how aligned are they? Are there historical legacies or different views about how power is expressed in the team and in the business?

Leadership teams recognize and appreciate the iceberg metaphor because it captures the dynamic between the material and non-material reality.

They say to me, "This summarizes our situation. We spend all of our time talking about the hard facts of our business (material reality) and nobody dares to talk about the issues that are under the water but those are the issues that are holding us back."

5.3 What Cows and Elephants Have in Common

There is language that warns us when we come close to those sensitive topics under the iceberg. The term, "sacred cow" is one of them. Literally, a sacred cow is an animal that is to be treated with reverence and respect. It is also a term used to describe a topic that is not discussable. It is out of bounds (at least out of the material reality); perhaps due to historical legacies or maybe it is connected to someone with a lot of power. In any case, when you hear someone say, "That's a sacred cow in this team," it is a warning to stay clear of the topic.

"When are we going to talk about the elephant in the room?", someone asked me recently at an off-site break. This is another term used to describe sensitive themes that are obvious, yet unresolved. Leaders who strive for high performance recognize that sacred cows and elephants in the room must be addressed to enable a team to play at its full potential. To leave these topics untouched discourages authentic exchange among team members and hinders resilient relationship building. This in turn slows down problem solving, reduces the speed and quality of decision-making and handicaps strategic change and execution.

As we discussed in Chap. 1, the impact of unmanaged or unresolved issues in the senior leadership team influences the entire organization. Performance source codes and the field of consequences compound matters because what is happening (or not) in the leadership team spreads throughout the rest of the organization.

Why executives do not address issues in the non-material reality: (Their words, not mine.)

(1) *"It is not my role—I am here to run part of this business, not be a psychologist."*
(2) *"It's not really that bad, I can still get my work done."*
(3) *"Isn't this the way things work at the executive level? Who said this was going to be easy? I thought all leadership teams ran this way."*
(4) *"I have never been very good with these soft issues; when things get emotional or touchy-feely."*
(5) *"If I share how I feel or reveal who I don't trust in this team, I will become very unpopular. It's better not to rock the boat."*

Leaders who cannot or will not discuss the "softer facts" of their business adopt coping strategies and practice "friendly avoidance" when the team touches on sensitive, non-material topics. Friendly and diplomatic amongst each other, leaders try to keep topics in the small, visible part of the iceberg that deals with the hard facts, steering clear of issues that have no clear cut answer and touch on people's emotions.

Yet politeness is the poison of effective collaboration. The cost of steering clear of non-material issues in your team means people pull back, and like the iceberg, only show a small part of who they are to the rest of the team. Conversations become artificial, real issues, conflicts, misunderstandings do not get addressed in a meaningful way, and thus the team performs at a reduced capacity. These practices are mirrored in the organization and performance and engagement suffer. When your business suffers, so does your customer experience.

You do not need to be in an executive leadership team to feel the submerged part of the iceberg. For instance; when you are in a meeting and the discussion begins to get heavy, you and others struggle; not because of the business complexity, but because the discussion touches on something that is considered taboo. You look around the room and see people attempting to stay on the discussion line; your intuition tells you that something "under the waterline" is the real issue but nobody wants to bring it up. Later in the day you hear people relate to this experience by saying, "there was an elephant in the room this morning." An outsider would not recognize this, but if you are an insider, you know what they mean.

The rational side of business rewards us for thinking and reminds us not to become "too emotional" in our business relationships. What a mistake and loss of potential when we are told, do not get emotional, after all, it is just business.

5.4 Respecting Both Realities

Creating alignment, mutual respect and trust in the non-material reality means learning to accept that how others see things might be different from how you see them. In the material reality, we reward debate and argue to see who is right. In the non-material reality, everyone is right because this reality is subjective; it is based on someone's perception. When a leader says she does not feel respected in the leadership team, who is to say she is wrong. Learning to accept, not argue in the non-material reality allows people to feel respected, not only for what they think, but also for what they feel.

The ability to work effectively in both the material and non-material reality is the hallmark of a leadership team that plays at their best. Above the iceberg, leaders use their business intelligence, analytic and strategic skills to be successful. Under the iceberg, in the non-material reality, leaders use their emotional competence, including listening skills and the ability to accept opinions and perceptions that may be different from their own.

The material reality thrives on an objective truth. The non-material reality thrives on an "emotional truth", individual perceptions which are personal and subjective in nature. Germans have a useful word for perception. They use the word *Wahrnehmung*. It is their word for perception, and it combines two other words, *Wahr*, which means "the truth" and *nehmen*, which means, "to take". Perception means, "The truth I take" from a particular situation. Imagine an executive meeting aimed at the future. Several members of the team propose innovative (yet untested) business models for the future.

This conversation may be inviting and energizing for some, but for others it may be uninteresting because it is not concrete enough. I often witness discussions like this in executive meetings. Different perceptions about how to manage the future effectively is not a problem in itself. It becomes a problem for this team if these different perceptions are not exchanged openly, appreciated and eventually aligned so that all members of the team can move forward with a common understanding of how they, as a leadership team, want to address the company's future together, the team's success will be limited.

5.5 Toolkit for Titanic Challenges

You do not find disturbances in the non-material reality on your company's balance sheet. Remember, they are under the water, out of sight and out of sound, meaning people do not talk about them openly. Steven Gaffney, a communication expert whose work I appreciate, says it like this, "The most important thing about communication is getting the unsaid, said." [2].

My role as an executive leadership consultant is not only to help leaders to recognize and express their imbalances in the non-material reality to me, but to openly address them to each other so they can start to work with it constructively.

Two ways to get leaders to "get the unsaid said" are during efforts we call *perception gatherings* and *experience visualizations*. Both are short processes that help leadership teams get under the iceberg quickly and effectively. Here is how the perception gathering works.

Perception Gatherings

The perception gathering resembles an open-ended interview process, conducted one on one with each member of the executive team. After gaining the commitment of the senior leader in the team, and after that leader has introduced me to the team, (either in meeting with the team or electronically) I will share the following with the group:

> Soon I will interview you and other members of your leadership team, as well as key stakeholders, in preparation for our first session together.
>
> The purpose of these conversations is for me to hear the experience of each you, and essentially your perception of where your business and strategy is today and ideas for improvement. This includes your vision for the future and areas where change needs to happen. This also allows me to begin building rapport with each of you before the off-site. This step is critical if we are to deal with fundamental or deeper issues in the face-to-face time the group will have at your executive ownershift sessions. The interviews provide a great opportunity for us to build a dimension of trust and understanding that will lead to open dialogue about the issues that will need to be faced in the future that lies ahead.
>
> Let me emphasize that these interviews are confidential in the sense that the details of what is disclosed by you is not shared by me in any way with other members of the organization. Who said what is not the point: I will be looking for commonly held views and themes.
>
> The confidentiality contract is maintained. Revisions and updates to the plan for the sessions will be made accordingly. I will distribute the consolidated perception summary to all team members during the opening session of your off-site. (The perception summary will be shared and discussed with the senior leader prior to the opening session) and will support any adaptations to final agenda setting process.

The open question format and the confidentially clause creates the security and the release for leaders to share what is really on their mind and in their hearts. Members of the team then allow me to consolidate the key messages from these interviews (anonymously of course) into the perception gathering consolidation. Key messages are captured verbatim, as long as I can preserve the confidentially clause, I do not include team members names, except for the senior leader in the team. Here I gather specific feedback for them, often using these questions:

> What's Sandra (the senior leader in the team) doing that is helpful and/or you appreciate?
>
> What could Sandra do differently that would enable you to be more effective or help the team succeed?

Once they have accepted and committed to the executive ownershift process, the senior leader of the team is eager to get this personal feedback as well as to show their willingness to "go first and show their vulnerability" in front of their leadership team. This sets the tone and the example for the degree of disclosure (which breeds trust) that Sandra expects in her leadership team.

The perception consolidation is comprised of comments coming directly from the members of the leadership team. I organize the comments according to common themes that surface, such as:

Team culture and dynamics
Team performance
Personal insights
Future direction and strategy
Business issues/structure and responsibilities
Leadership
Expectations/desired outcomes.

The personal comments reflect the "emotional truths" and present the feelings and perceptions of the leadership team members. We discuss the contents openly and the team then builds their executive ownershift growth agenda from what they believe is important to address and change in their business. Leaders are grateful for the support to get their submerged issues on the table, so they can be transformed into competitive assets for their team and their organization.

As discussed earlier, you do not have to be in an executive team to be sunk by the submerged part of the iceberg. One only has to look at a long line of failed business integrations (BMW Rover, Daimler Chrysler, Lucent Alcatel, Sprint Nextel to name a few) to remember that business mergers that executives proclaim as "made in heaven" often end in the "fiery pits of dysfunction," because they did not learn to merge their non-material realities of trust, respect and power. (You can look into the reason for these failures with multiple publications such as the Harvard Business Review who stated about Daimler Chrysler: "[The merger failed] … because the two organizations really didn't like each other, and couldn't cooperate to the extent necessary to make the combination work." [3].

It is important to remind an executive team that is considering an acquisition that every merger occurs three times. Once as a legal agreement (stock swap, valuation and purchase price), the rational merger (new org structures that help everyone find their new place) and the emotional merger, where executives and employees own the belief and practice that cooperation has a higher value than competing with each other.

Merging businesses or enabling business functions to work together to serve clients effectively require larger groups of people to manage their non-material realities respectfully and constructively.

Experience Visualizations

Visualizing how people experience working collaborations is an alternative to the perception gathering tool I shared earlier. Especially for larger populations, where individual conversations and interviews might be too time consuming, experience visualizations quickly help to understand where blockages in the non-material reality exist between people, functions and businesses. Asking subgroups to visualize (yes, this means painting) how they experience their collaboration with others is an efficient way to identify disturbances in the non-material reality. Jochen Peter Breuer and Pierre de Bartha, experts in building highly effective global business collaborations, help transform interpersonal and intercultural differences into competitive assets through a process called the mental merger [4].

In their work, non-material disturbances can be quickly identified (what they call emotional viruses) and transformed into positive messages. Through dozens of global business collaborations, Breuer and Bartha have been able to help different types of organizations learn to work together by appreciating and leveraging complimentary differences. They are true pioneers in the field of collective emotional intelligence and I have profited tremendously from our work together. Breuer has expanded on this work and today helps leaders create psychological safety in organizations, practice relationship simplexity, and effectively manage collective emotions.

Leadership teams and groups that understand the leadership reality iceberg and are eager to play at their best are motivated to explore and improve misalignments in the non-material reality. As mentioned earlier, Breuer and Bartha use the term emotional viruses to describe key player relationships that are infected by misperceptions. The resulting effect for one or more of the people involved can be aggressive behavior, disrespectful communication or avoidance strategies. All of these set a poor example for the rest of the organization. Leaders who feel that they can camouflage their real feelings and act as if everything is fine are sadly mistaken. People are quick to feel when leaders do not behave authentically, and while they may not say so publicly, they begin to model the behavior they learn from others. These are not the practices of an organization that strives to play at their best.

Relationship Mapping

Relationship mapping helps executive teams understand how others in the team see their working relationships. This helps build resilient relationships that stand in good times and bad times. Part of the leadership team will place the names of all the leadership team members in a large circle on the board and then are given three pens: green, black and red (Fig. 5.2).

I ask them to draw lines and connect the senior leaders as to how they perceive the relationship they have with each other. If they feel two leadership members have a constructive, trusting relationship, they draw a green line between the two leaders. If they are not sure about the relationship, they draw a black line between the two people. If the group feels the two people have a misalignment, different perceptions on key issues and they are not communicating respectively and constructively with each other, they draw a red line. Having a red line between leaders does not mean they do not work together; it is that others see the relationship as not operating

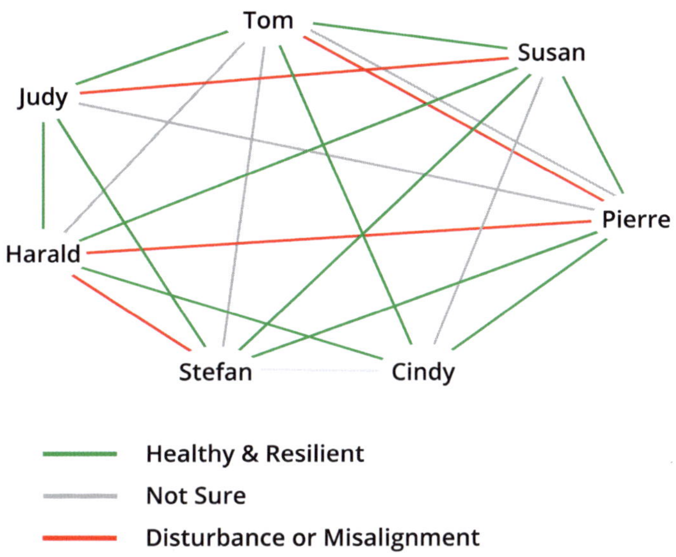

Fig. 5.2 Relationship mapping

optimally. This process takes place in a confidential setting, only shared and discussed between the leadership team.

Relationship mapping can become the starting point to reset key player relationships.

Unwritten Rules and Hidden Agendas

Unwritten rules, sometimes called hidden agendas, may be mentioned in the perception gathering or amongst leaders. Another useful exercise is to ask leaders to describe the unwritten rules that exist in their team. What are the taboo topics that people feel but do not speak about? While some teams struggle initially with this; once reminded that the path playing at their best means rebalancing and aligning the non-material reality, people are forthcoming.

I remind leadership teams that emotional viruses, unwritten rules and even hidden agendas only have power when they remain under the water. (Under the water means not discussed openly and constructively.) Once exposed, through visualization, relationship mapping or simply writing them down, teams begin to take positive steps forward.

Often I let the non-material disclosures sit with the group for an evening or a day, giving people the opportunity to connect with someone where an imbalance may exist. After allowing some time for these non-material disclosures to surface, we return to them and the team discusses how they would like to operate in the future, taking into account their non-material reality experiences. This leads to team rules, or standards of excellence that address material and non-material expectations between key players. Commitments to stay accountable to these team practices helps the team to play at its best.

Let us be clear—a high performing leadership team or organization constantly deals with differences and conflicts of different sorts. What separates the mediocre from those teams that play at their best is their willingness and openness to deal with their Titanic challenges.

Leaders can tap into phenomenal amounts of positive well-being and improved clarity and understanding between people and teams when they delve into the "under the iceberg issues." Creating an environment where people can express their perceptions or emotional truths enables people to bring their "whole self" into the job, team and organization. Anything is possible in an environment that is inclusive and respectful. This is what team spirit is all about. Leaders who learn to reown both leadership realities stand out.

There is not anything that can undo the Titanic tragedy, but it can be a powerful and long lasting lesson for leadership teams that want to drive their executive ownershift.

References

1. Breuer, J. P., & Frot, P. (2012). *Das emotionale Unternehmen: Mental starke Organisationen entwickeln—Emotionale Viren aufspüren und behandeln* (German). Germany: Springer Gabler.
2. Gaffney, S. (2002). *Just be honest: Authentic communication strategies that get results and last a lifetime.* Coral Springs, FL: JMG Publishing.
3. Watkins, M. D. (2007, May). *Why DaimlerChrysler Never Got into Gear.* Brighton, MA: Harvard Business Review.
4. Breuer, J. P., & de Bartha, P. (2012). *Deutsch-Französische Geschäftsbeziehungen erfolgreich managen. Spielregeln für die Zusammenarbeit auf Führungs—und Fachebene* [How to Successfully Manage German-French Business Relationships. Guidelines for Working Together at the Leadership and Expert Level]. Germany: Gabler Springer Publishing Group.

6 Making Meetings Matter

The way you do anything is the way you do everything.
—Tom Waits

6.1 The Indian Wedding

They were a young couple in love. Their parents could not have been prouder. Both families wanted the wedding celebration to be the finest and grandest the village had ever seen, however both families were poor beyond description.

The families came up with an idea. They would put their meager resources together and bring an exquisite feast to everyone in the village. They asked all the guests to bring a flask of red wine and everyone agreed. The proud parents assured everyone that they would manage the rest.

The wedding day finally arrived and marital vows were exchanged as the parents and everyone in the village watched. After the ceremony, bride, groom and parents stood at the front of the reception line and greeted everyone. Afterwards each guest moved past the greeting line and poured the contents of their humble clay containers into the huge celebration urn for all to later enjoy.

After greeting the last guest, the proud fathers of the bride and groom took their wine glasses and dipped them together deep into the clay wine urn to toast to the couple's new future together and to say thank you to all the guests for coming and contributing.

As the two men brought their glasses out of the urn, everyone realized that their glasses were not filled with red wine. Their glasses were clear and filled with water.

The proud moment turned to sadness, and looking out amongst the guests, everyone realized they had played a part in turning a wonderful celebration into a shameful example of what happens when people do not deliver on their promises.

D. Norenberg, *Executive Ownershift*, Management for Professionals,
https://doi.org/10.1007/978-3-030-35828-0_6

Each of the guests had thought, 'nobody will notice if my flask is filled with water, as all the others will bring wine.' Yet that was the thinking of all the guests, each believing that if they did not do their part, nobody would notice.

It was a terribly sad and embarrassing moment for everyone; a lesson the village never forgot.

This is an important story for all of us that attend and lead meetings. It is a gentle reminder of what can happen when we fail to recognize how important our contribution is to each meeting we attend. It is easy to make a full contribution to meetings that we lead ourselves or where we have something important at stake. However, if we are honest with ourselves, can each of us say that we bring "our full contribution" to each and every meeting that we participate in?

6.2 Value Generator or Cost Sinkhole?

When meetings are not organized properly, people are not prepared, the right people are not present, or there is little sense of urgency to use the meeting as a catalyst for improvement and growth, the costs are staggering [1]. See for yourself:

- 37 billion dollars is wasted in meetings annually.
- More than 50% of an executive's time is spent in meetings and these same executives consider 67% of the meetings they attend as failures.
- The more meetings people attend, the more exhausted they feel and the higher they perceive their workload to be.
- The meeting costs for a company with 1000 employees is nearly 2.5 million dollars per year.
- 25% of meeting time is spent discussing irrelevant issues.
- A recent survey showed that 92% of people confessed to multitasking during meetings, whether checking email or doing other work that is not related to the meeting at hand.

When I ask executives and senior leaders to tell me about the quality and results that come from the meetings that they lead, their initial responses sound like this:

> Dan, I've been running meetings for 25 years so this isn't an area where you are going to tell me anything new.
>
> We have an HR initiative to help our first time managers run better meetings, so we have that covered.
>
> Our meetings, well I guess they are ok, you know, one of the necessary evils of being a top leader.
>
> Nobody really complains about them.

Even as they share these comments, most executives know the importance of their leadership meeting and the impact it has on the rest of the business. Knowing is not doing. This distance between knowing and doing is the combination of focusing on what is essential, practicing discipline and being accountable.

Sometimes the hectic and overwhelming executive demands give leaders reason to believe that highly effective meetings will simply happen if they show up. Meetings and all the demands around meetings can look like an obligation instead of an opportunity.

The feedback I collect in the perception gathering (Chap. 5) helps reposition the importance of making meetings matter in the team's executive agenda.

Here are selected comments from several different leadership teams. See for yourself what is below the water:

> We need a clear goal for our leadership meetings.
>
> There are certain topics that can only be addressed in this leadership meeting. If they do not get on our agenda our growth plan and our future success will suffer.
>
> Sometimes prep materials do not arrive in time and other times we simply aren't prepared to discuss the topics in the detail needed. The consequences can lead us to make decisions that are not really on a solid foundation, or we postpone issues, again and again.
>
> What are our acceptable norms for working well with each other? We don't need to dig up the past but we do need to be clear about this for the future.
>
> We are far too nice, too polite in the way we interact with each other at our leadership meeting. We need to develop a more aggressive position if we expect to be successful.
>
> Our leadership meetings are very strict; you do not really feel at ease during the meeting.
>
> We don't benefit from the experience of the others – this is a pity as there are smart guys in the room.
>
> I'm missing the real engagement in our leadership meeting. I get the impression that everyone is working for himself – with his aims, challenges with little interest in issues.
>
> You have to be careful if you challenge something outside of your area of responsibility, people start to get defensive if you question things outside of your area.
>
> I am unlikely to bring a problem into this leadership meeting if I am made to feel stupid by the way another member responds to me or my issue.
>
> The executive leadership meeting is not a platform for us to show off as to how good we are.

How many of these statements are consistent with experiences in your team?

Improving your leadership meetings is not rocket science, but it does require purposeful intent, courageous engagement, flexibility and disciplined follow through.

It does not matter who you are or what business you are in, everyone can create improvements in their leadership meetings.

6.3 Define Your Meeting

The question that you and members of your leadership team should be eager to answer is:

"Why is our leadership meeting the best meeting in the company?"

If you and your leadership team cannot answer that question with clarity and alignment, start here:

"What do we need to do, as a leadership team, to run the most effective meetings in our company?"

Does your leadership meeting need to be the best in the company? Maybe not, but at least it better be in the top 10%.

Who sets the gold standard for highly effective meetings in your business? If it is not the executive or senior leadership team of a particular business, who does it?

6.4 Chaos in the Executive Committee

"The Executive Committee meets twice a year, managing executive and strategic issues and making decisions to guide their two billion dollar technology company in a tough market with competitors many times their size. The CEO is looking for support for himself and his team."

The thought of advising and coaching a committee was not my favorite idea. "A committee is a group that keeps minutes and loses hours," comedian Milton Berle once said. I was not sure to what degree this definition fit with the executive group in question.

The CEO asked me to help him strengthen his leadership team, including the collaboration and performance in the executive committee meeting.

We agreed that our starting point would be to observe their executive committee meeting. I would provide my initial insights into how the team managed this experience, and explore the implications this had in their business.

At the London executive committee meeting, I observed how team members collaborated with one another and how they engaged with their strategic topics on the agenda. Yet rather than share my first impressions initially after the meeting, we set up a learning reflection to get these executives talking about how they experienced their meeting.

By engaging them, they reflect, when they reflect, they learn and make choices that help the team improve.

After their comments, I asked three questions.

(1) Who was the moderator or the chair of today's management meeting? __________

(2) On a scale of one to ten, with ten being exceptional, how would you rate the results, decisions and actions agreed upon in this meeting? __________

(3) On a scale of one to ten, with ten being very high and one being very low, how would you rank the way you, as a team, managed the relationships and the creative energy in this meeting? __________

I asked for their answers on a card, collecting the data anonymously, and suggested they take a coffee break. When they returned, I shared the results with them:

> To the question, *who was the meeting moderator* for this thirteen-member leadership committee – there were five different people named as the moderator, including the CEO.
>
> To the question about *results, decisions and actions,* their average score was 5.6.
>
> To the question about *relationships and energy*, their average score was 6.

After sharing the results with them, a constructive discussion followed about what was working and was not working in this leadership meeting.

The leaders "owned up" that their leadership meetings was not as effective as it could be. We explored the implications this had for the leadership team and for their overall business.

I asked, "What's one thing that this team could do differently in the next meeting to improve both the results and the relationship energy in this meeting?"

The leaders identified the following actions and agreed to follow through on:

- Better time management, pay closer attention to the time for topics
- Develop rules of interaction
- Establish decision-making criteria
- Develop a constructive feedback climate
- Clarify the role of the moderator.

Over time, team effectiveness improved and so did execution on strategic initiatives in the executive committee, which was renamed the "Leadership Team" shortly thereafter. The Leadership Team embraced a new style of reflection, discussion and follow through process and this helped the team create a more aligned and distinct team identity and results driven structure. The most distinct difference for this team six months later, from my point of view, was that they moved from conversations from talking about what was broken to conversations about what was possible. Their *ownershift* was activated.

6.5 Setting the Stage for Meetings that Matter

Observing leadership meetings gives me a very clear picture of what is going on in an organization. This is one of the fastest and most effective ways to learn how a company operates.

I have observed and facilitated hundreds of business meetings over the past twenty years. From coaching global investment firms on how to run daily 20-minute investment update meetings to facilitating business transformation initiatives to advising billion-dollar management boards how to run meetings that are more meaningful.

Six insights to help you lead meetings that matter:

1. As a leader, a fundamental part of your executive agenda is developing and leading highly effective meetings. There is no way out of this.
2. Regardless of how much experience you have, planning and leading meaningful meetings for your team is one of the most difficult jobs that any leader faces.
3. Even if your meetings are highly effective today, this is no guarantee that they will be effective in the future, meaning that you have to constantly adjust and adapt with the times.
4. Your management team members will have different expectations of what makes an effective meeting. (Always listen, consider the different points of view and make choices how to address the needs of the team, the business and your customers.)
5. Creating and leading meetings that matter is the single most important tool you have to engage people toward leading meaningful change and create breakthrough results in your business.
6. What happens in your leadership meeting happens in your business, multiplied many times over. What happens in the executive meeting impacts everyone in the company, including your customers.

Here are fundamentals I look for:

- Has the agenda been circulated beforehand, clearly outlining the pre-reads and what is expected of them for each of the agenda topics? (Information exchange, problem solving, decision-making, thoughtful exchange.)
- Does the meeting start on time?
- Is there an effective follow-up process on strategic topics from their previous meetings, results driven not just a discussion of activities, as well as solid consequences in place for performance and non-performance?
- Do the meeting members give the impression that they are prepared for the topics, discussions, problems they want to solve and the decisions they intend to make?
- Do leaders share their struggles and challenges in the team; enabling them to get help from other leaders in the team?
- Is there a climate of creative tension and constructive conflict in this leadership team or is it a polite, diplomatic country club environment where people make jokes rather than address difficult issues?

Do the members of this executive meeting walk out with:

- more clarity regarding their business mission and strategy?
- deeper emotional connection to their team members and their strategy?
- a more cohesive and aligned team of leaders?
- the impression that they enjoy what they do in the leadership meeting?

The executive leadership meeting is where leadership teams give birth to their company culture. The leadership meeting is the incubator for performance throughout the organization.

If you see things in your organization that frustrate you or shouldn't happen, I can show you how the performance source code (Chap. 1) starts or is tolerated in executive meetings.

If your meetings do not start on time, you will see that your organization does not deliver key projects on time. If your meetings do not have a reputation or a record for decision making, problem solving and resource allocation where needed, you will not find a real sense of urgency in your organizational culture.

Use leadership meetings to promote best practices and identify blockages in cross- functional collaboration. Let leaders use these meetings as a learning resource for their wicked problems. If your meetings are not addressing such topics, spend time in your next meeting working on how to create more impact in your executive meetings.

Does your executive meeting have to be the best meeting in the company? If it is not, you have some explaining to do to your staff about why the highest paid, most influential team in the company does not set the example for others to follow. Visit other meetings, both inside and outside the company to learn how others make the most of their meetings.

Make your meetings matter, because they do.

6.6 Leadership Meeting Field Notes

Many of consulting and coaching clients start with my Executive Team Make-Meetings-Matter-Package (MMMP). This one-day session helps leadership teams experience first-hand how quickly *executive ownershift* can start producing results for them. Leadership teams take tremendous value from these sessions. Should they choose to work with me on more significant projects within 90 days of our initial engagement, the one-day meeting observation and feedback session is credited to their follow up projects.

Leaders appreciate getting immediate feedback and suggestions after their leadership meetings, delivered to them, face to face. The fresh feedback enables them to make choices for immediate improvement, in their leadership team and other teams that they oversee. My observation notes and ideas are typed up and given to the entire team within 48 hour session.

Here is a sample of what this feedback, taken from actual leadership meetings, looks like:

Getting started

Consider in the opening round asking everyone for a short statement about what's important for them today. The answers could range from a desired business result or something like, "I want to see us have an engaging and respectful discussion like we did at our last meeting." It gets everyone awake and involved right away and then the person leading the meeting has a feel for the climate and topics on people's mind.

Create a strategic agenda

An agenda is more than a list of topics; by addressing the most important things first, you set the tone as the senior leadership team. Clarifying whether the topics are for information giving, solving problems or reaching a decision helps team members know what is expected of them.

Be conscious of talk time

Who talked during this meeting? If it is mainly one person, consider changing the format to create more involvement. Remember, involvement breeds commitment.

Decisions Score

At the end of each meeting, ask, "What decisions did we make at this meeting?" Keep score and improve your results. Decisions drive business success.

Talking-Questioning-Listening-Interrupting

What was the best question(s) in your last meeting? Questions invite leaders to think and take ownership of issues. Use questions to bring strategic thinking into this senior leadership team.

Be brief and come to the point

There is a saying amongst jazz musicians—do not make it up if it doesn't help. In the age of information overload, you will become a more effective leader when you are brief and come to the point. If the point has been made, there is no need to repeat the same information over it.

Compliments and Critique

Does your meeting culture encourage people to share their struggles and for others to want to help and support, rather than judge? Ask for some healthy critique from your colleagues and use it to improve. High performance executive meetings balance compliments and praise with critique. Start keeping score to stay conscious of this important insight.

Map complex issues

Visualizing or mapping a complex topic enables everyone to see a common picture of the situation, enabling everyone to work together to resolve the issues and move the plan forward. Visualizing complex topics helps clarify:

- What are the key issues here?
- What is our timeline?
- Who manages the risk/reward analysis of the different options available to us?
- What does an issue map look like here? (Shows key issues and how they are linked to one another.)

Finding a Diamond Requires Some Digging

When Harold shared that his business unit is the innovation driver in the market, nobody asked for details. I want to know what he is doing to make this claim and take his ideas back to my team for review. Even if his approach doesn't match to my business, I have at least challenged my team in a conversation that is strategic and growth driven. Dig for your diamonds.

Share your struggles

Good exchange opportunities are here. Use the intellectual firepower and years of business wisdom in this executive team to get ideas for your struggles and perhaps a big idea for business breakthroughs and growth.

Start by:

Sharing something that you are struggling with and ask for help.

As well as:

Ask at the end of each review, if you had one suggestion or idea for my business, what would it be?

This will create a wealth of ideas that you can review with your teams. All of you are good at what you do; you can become better (and you must become better) if you tap into the vast wisdom of this team.

The suggestions should be short and provocative, write them down on a flip chart and then detailed discussions can follow later where appropriate. There is no need for defensive behavior or ego protection in this round. When one of you gets an idea that helps a part of the business, you all win.

6.7 Standards of Excellence

What is a highly effective meeting in your team's eyes? What are the best practices that your leadership team members have gathered over the years? What are the standards of excellence, sometimes called team rules that guide how your meetings run and what topics you deal with and what topics you do not deal with.

You cannot become an excellent team if you don't learn how to run excellent meetings, and you don't run excellent meetings if you don't have standards of excellence for your team meetings. Standards of excellence hold people accountable and let people know what is expected of them. Again, these meeting rules do not need to be overcomplicated, start with the basics and you can adapt the rules over time. Here are some examples from previous teams:

- Attendance is mandatory
- One discussion going at one time
- No cell phones
- No presentations by subordinates
- Questions are valued and appreciated in our meetings so ask them
- Every agenda item is identified as to how the team will work with it. (Discussion, decision, problem solving, brainstorming)

From my experience with over 100 leadership teams, standards of excellence differ from team to team. They can clarify the meeting purpose, structure, timing, roles and rules of engagement. What is most important is that you work on them together to create an aligned approach to what makes a meeting matter to you and the team. Then hold each other accountable.

6.8 Meeting Performance Catalysts

Meeting performance catalysts enable you to create a constructive climate and boost results in your meetings via specific measures. Here are some that really add a kick to your meeting effectiveness.

Creating Soft and Hard Space

Successful leadership teams create soft and hard space in their leadership meetings. This means creating an empathetic (soft) atmosphere where people feel safe to bring their fears, concerns and aspirations into the team space. This comes through intentional listening, good questions and looking at issues from different points of view.

Teams balance this soft space with a hard space, this means practicing integrity and putting tough issues on the table (even if they impact your function negatively but you know it's better for the overall business), following through on decisions and holding each other accountable for behaviors you've agreed on.

Customers at Every Meeting

Practice putting your customer in every meeting. Place an empty chair in every meeting room. This chair represents your customer. As discussions get heated and people fall back into their favorite positions to protect personal interests and turf, turn to the customer chair and ask, what choices should we make that would best serve our customer?

Mental Preparation Makes Meetings Matter

There is a great deal of energy that goes into your meeting preparation. The success of this meeting is partly about the themes you select, the pre-reading and your ability to take decisions. Yet it is the mental preparation that costs nothing and gives us the extra edge.

Use these three questions, or some of your own, to mentally prepare yourself to play your best before the next leadership meeting:

Why is this going to be a very effective meeting in the morning?
How can I participate to make our meeting a success?
What specifically do I need to contribute or get from this meeting for it to be effective and worthwhile for me?

Creating a Culture of Continuous Improvement

What is it like to work for a company that improves every day? You can be part of creating a company like this when you insist on continuous improvement in your leadership meetings.

At the end of every executive meeting, gather feedback as to what worked well or what you could do differently next time around. This can be done by asking people (use a card if you want) to rank the effectiveness of the business results achieved during the session (10 is excellent, 1 you wished you'd never attended). Then ask the leaders to rate the quality of collaboration during the meeting. (10 is highly collaborative, open and trustful, 1 means the meeting resembled a group of Roman gladiators battling it out). Close by asking, what's the one thing we can do to make our meetings more results-oriented and collaborative in the future?

In Fig. 6.1, we see how the y axis (vertical line) measures how people experienced the business results generated in the meeting. The x axis (horizontal line) measures how people experienced the collaboration climate in the meeting. Ask people to place their dot that describes their experience and then discuss ways to improve at the next meeting.

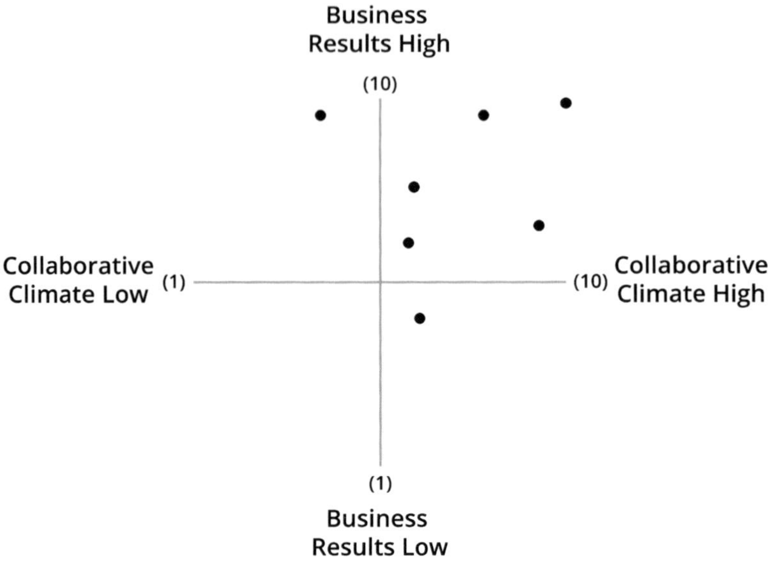

Fig. 6.1 Continuous improvement visual

6.9 Your Contribution Counts

Reflecting on this making meeting matter chapter and how every leader contributes to a meeting's climate and results reminds me of an experience I had in high school. It was during the August two-a-day football practices, going into my senior year of high school. We had a very good team, ranked to do well in the state that year and I was leading the team as the quarterback, the playmaker as many call this position.

What else could a seventeen year old ask for, playing quarterback for his hometown in his senior and final year of high school? Looking back now, I can see that my head was way up in the clouds.

School had not started yet and we had just finished another brutal practice in the Iowa August sun, when the coaches called all the seniors into a room for a special meeting.

"Maybe some reporters are here and want to speak to a few of us," I reasoned.

After we all got in the room, the coaching staff took turns sharing with us what was at stake for the season, and that for many people in the room, who would not go on and play football in college, this was the last time that they would ever put on a football uniform and play for a team. Our best contributions were expected, the coaches reminded us.

This all was fine and well, however I didn't see what this had to do with me when Mike Myers, the quarterback and receiver coach turned to me and said, "And what about you Norenberg?"

I sat up in my chair and asked, "What do you mean Coach?"

Perhaps it was my naïve reply, or the blistering heat that affected Coach Myers, but he turned to me and with the force of fury shouted, "We have been out in the sun for two hours, running drills to get all of you ready as a team for the season opener in two weeks. Where are you, Norenberg, in all of these drills? I will tell you where you are, you are in the middle of the pack, running behind sophomores and juniors and you are supposed to be one of the leaders of this team. You are hiding in the middle. What kind of leadership is that?"

I felt about two inches tall. I had mistakenly thought that as the quarterback I could cruise through the drills, minimize my contribution and keep myself fresh for the scrimmage sessions. In other words, I was not making the leadership contribution that he expected of me.

I learned my lesson that day and have made it my business to pass this lesson on to leaders that work with me.

There is too much cruising in senior leadership meetings. Not only do executives miss opportunities to accelerate the impact of their leadership decisions in the business, they set a "cruising culture" for everyone else in the organization. This costs your business huge amounts of money and gives competitors that make meetings matter an advantage over you that need not be.

The way you do anything is the way you do everything. This means the way your meetings run is the way your business runs.

Make the *executive ownershift* and start acting this way.

Reference

1. Kolowich, L. (2014, August). *The ugly truth about meetings*. https://blog.hubspot.com/marketing/ugly-truth-about-meetings-infographic.

Superficial Versus Senseful Strategy 7

For if the trumpet give an uncertain sound,
who shall prepare himself for the battle?
—I Corinthians 14.8

7.1 Superficial Strategy

Creating, implementing and executing business strategy is the responsibility of the executive team or senior leadership team for their site, function or company. While there are many activities that leadership teams can delegate to others, strategy is not one of them. Few leadership teams disagree with this, and most believe they are doing their best to be successful. Results, however, show that few actually deliver:

- Only 10% of formulated strategy actually is executed successfully.
- 85% of management teams spend less than one hour a month on strategy issues.
- Only 5% of employees understand their corporate strategy.
- Only 2% of leaders surveyed are confident that they will achieve 80–100% of their strategy's objectives [1].

When we look into the situations that support these statistics, we see that leadership teams struggle because they have settled (most of the time unknowingly) for a superficial strategy.

I have never met a leadership team that liked to hear their strategy described this way. Yet when leaders are honest, vulnerable and speak openly about how strategy works (and does not work) in their organization, they often admit that something is missing.

D. Norenberg, *Executive Ownershift*, Management for Professionals,
https://doi.org/10.1007/978-3-030-35828-0_7

Strategy that does not perform beyond expectations is superficial. It is strategy that is missing the mark. This could be because it is not rationally clear, emotionally engaging, or compelling people to collaborate effectively.

I give leadership teams this language when they express disappointment with their strategy or their strategic results. Stop blaming others in your organization, the lack of resources, the conditions in the marketplace, or your competitors, all familiar scapegoats when strategy does not go as planned. Simply acknowledging that you have a superficial strategy provokes a great deal of reactions, from talented leaders who are used to succeeding at everything they do.

The phrase superficial strategy stings. Many take issue with the implication. Others feel a desire to defend their team. Yet when leaders accept this language, superficial strategy, and make it their own to describe the shortcoming in their strategy, it serves as a catalyst that encourages an *executive ownershift* in how they engage with their strategy and their organization.

Leadership teams fall short of their strategic ambitions, in many instances, because they settle for strategy authorship, rather than strategic ownership. Just because a leadership team has created strategy (authorship) *does not mean they and the organization own it.*

If the leadership team does not rationally and emotionally own the strategy, how can anyone else in the organization be expected to own it. The way strategy works or does not work in your organization is directly related to how strategy is created and led by the executive team.

This is the difference between "superficial strategy" and "senseful strategy." A senseful strategy is one that people see as rationally clear, emotionally compelling and calls them to high levels of collaboration to deliver on it with a sense of individual and collective ownership.

The Dilbert cartoon may not represent the conversation in your executive team. However, if your strategy is not rationally clear, purposeful for those at all levels of the organization or does not compel people to collaborate effectively with one another for your company's success, this is the conversation that people use to express how they experience *superficial* strategy.

7.2 Senseful Strategy as a Sixth Sense

The opposite of a superficial strategy is a senseful strategy. Senseful is seldom used in the English language, and the term senseful strategy is even more rare, unless of course, you are well versed in the language of *executive ownershift*. Senseful means purposeful and significant, brimming with sense; and strategy is the framework that allows you to make decisions that support the nature and direction of your business [2].

Sense, by definition, is the physical power that makes it possible to know about things outside of our mind and body. Think about the implications of this as it relates to strategy. Imagine everyone in your organization knows and feels the sense of your strategy and why it is essential that people work together to achieve it. This is strategy as a sixth sense.

A senseful strategy is purposeful, significant and full of sense, *enabling you and everyone else in the organization* to make choices and take decisions that support the nature and direction of your business.

Therefore, when your strategy is purposeful, significant and full of sense, you invite people to deeply engage themselves and become owners of what they do, because they are clear and connected to why they do it and have the freedom to pursue how they do it.

Leadership teams that invest in a senseful strategy create fertile ground for ownership. This is the deepest level of human engagement, beyond feeling responsible or being made accountable for something by somebody.

Ownership in this sense is not to be confused with physical ownership or to possess material things. Ownership to an ideal, a higher purpose or strategy says, *"We have a clear picture of how this will develop in the future, we are fully behind this path and we are confident that it is a journey worth taking."*

A senseful strategy enables a culture of ownership in your company. This ownership culture of deeply aligned purpose and engagement is what leads to remarkable results. This is core to the executive ownershift process. Too often leadership teams, disappointed with their results, change their strategy *without ever truly owning it*. This leads to patterns of mediocre performance that continues unless leadership teams get to the heart of the issue—crafting and leading by example a senseful strategy.

How do you evaluate your strategy performance unless you practice it with the full ownership of your leadership team and organization?

7.3 Five Elements of Senseful Strategy

There are five elements of a senseful strategy. They are:

1. Clarity
2. Connection
3. Collaboration
4. Contribution
5. Consequences

Use the following statements at your next leadership meeting to see to what degree your leadership team and your organization live the five elements. Better yet, to get a more comprehensive picture of how senseful strategy lives throughout your organization, take a cross section of leaders and individual contributors at different levels across your business to understand how others experience strategy at their level. As you read the following statements, give yourself a *ten* if you strongly agree with the statement, a *one* if you strongly disagree or other values in between.

1. **Clarity**

   - There is a common understanding in the executive team and throughout the organization of what our success looks like in three years.
   - Executive leaders are aligned to our future direction and priorities of both their business and our overall business, supporting each other's success.
   - There is a clear sense of why our strategy is meaningful, beyond financial results or simply growing faster than the market.

2. **Connection**

   - Members of our leadership team share their story and take a personal stand, one that expresses their ownership to the overall strategy.
   - The ownership culture practiced in the executive team motivates people throughout our organization to act like owners in our strategy.
   - There is an open climate to discuss concerns, doubts and questions about strategic topics, both in our executive team and throughout our organization.

3. **Collaboration**

   - Our executives work together in such a way that it serves as the compelling source for highly collaborative practices throughout our organization.
   - Effective collaborations (cross-site, cross-function) are benchmarked and shared across our business and poorly performing collaborations and bottlenecks are quickly addressed and improved.

- People in our organization, at all levels, are rewarded for demonstrating collaborative excellence.

4. **Contribution**

- People see how their contributions support our strategy and our success.
- There is a strong willingness, supported by deliberate practices at the senior leadership level, to stop or abandon activities that no longer contribute to strategic success, throughout the organization.
- We, as a leadership team and as an organization, recognize and appreciate successes that come from business areas other than our own.

5. **Consequences**

- There is a positive practice of acknowledging and celebrating successes throughout our organization, both individually and collectively.
- Our organization profits from our exceptional feedback culture, which is driven by the everyday practices in the executive team.
- Our customers serve as evangelists for us, acknowledging and promoting the value and benefits that our senseful strategy delivers to them. In other words, our customers feel they are at the center of everything we do.

7.4 Senseful Strategy Scorecard

135–150	**Congratulations. An excellent situation**, however remember that at this state, complacency sets in quickly. Continue to challenge yourself and your organization
120–134	**Good results, as a starting point**. Consider an "outside in" perspective, that is, if you were outside the organization looking in, what is missing to go to the next level?
100–119	**You are riding the fence**. You can point to strategic successes, but do not overlook areas for improvement. Give space to the critical voices in your organization, they believe you can do better than you are doing
80–99	**You are struggling**. Stop trying to do more of the same. It is time to step off the hectic treadmill and reset the senseful compass of strategy. Start now before you fall off the cliff
Less than 80	**You are in trouble**. If you see things differently, proceed at your own peril. Otherwise, breathe deeply and review what the five elements could truly mean for your team and your organization if you deeply embraced them

If your leadership team and your organization rate the five elements highly, you are among the select few who have learned to craft and lead a senseful strategy that encourages and supports an ownership culture.

7.5 Superficial to Senseful Pivots

The battle between the forces for a senseful strategy or a superficial strategy takes place in the senior leadership team. Sometimes this battle is direct and confrontational, others times it occurs by legacy, gradualism or complacency. Yet when leadership teams express disappointment, frustration or anger about how strategy is not performing in their organization, they need reminding that these consequences are the result of discussions and decisions (or lack of) taking place in the executive team.

Leadership teams learn to recognize and act on turning point moments, or pivots, during their strategic dialog and practice. A pivot is the point of importance, which everything else based on, when used as a noun. If something pivots, as a verb, it balances or turns on that central point. Pivots offer leadership teams the opportunity to move from one path to another, to pivot from a superficial path to a senseful path, when *executive ownershift* is present.

Now aware of the five elements (clarity, connection, collaboration, contribution and consequences) leadership teams can significantly influence the nature, direction and spirit of their strategy. Managed effectively, these pivots can serve as catalysts to breakthrough performance.

Here are statements from executive team exchanges that lead to superficial strategy; followed by ways to help leaders successfully manage their pivot. Which of these pivot points relate to something in your organization? Use situations like these as a starting point for reflection and renewal at your next executive team meeting or feel free to contact me if you would like some outside expertise to support you.

> Our strategy is numbers driven – we don't really engage with what we want our business to look like in two or three years. Our strategy is tactical and we have our nose very close to the ground. If we continue to work in the future as we do today, our business is at risk.

Business thrives on numbers but most people do not. We need numbers to help us measure progress and results in our business, but numbers alone will not stimulate a culture of ownership. Leaders often resort to number-driven plans, with the intention of creating clarity. In a senseful strategy, purpose is clear and the reasons for change (strategy) are imperative to survive and thrive. You have to know your business, and this means knowing your numbers, yet no amount of numbers can outperform a clear and compelling purpose.

What is the purpose of your strategy? What are the opportunities that you want to capitalize or the challenges that could become critical if you do not move to create a new future for your business? Why do you, as a business, exist and what are the contributions you intend to make that create value for your customers and the marketplace?

These are fundamental questions that enable you to create an attractive purpose, one that becomes contagious if people in your organization think and feel

- That you and the leadership team own your mission and strategy.
- Convinced that they are invited to participate with their full talents.
- That the strategic journey that you are inviting them on is achievable.

We are not clear about who does what around here,

so how are we are supposed to contribute to the overall strategy, this is just paralyzing us.

Unclarity and uncertainty are as much a part of life as they are a part of strategy. The key to a senseful strategy is to "manage out or manage down" unclarity regarding future direction, strategic priorities, and roles and responsibilities as much as possible. You cannot practice collaboration excellence without clarity in these areas.

Here are three ways for leadership teams to vacuum out the unclarity, and by doing so, enable highly collaborative cultures to flourish in your organization.

Questions Our Strategy Should Answer

This is a helpful discussion at the beginning of a strategic renewal process and during regular intervals on your strategic journey. Ask members of your leadership team or even a larger audience of leaders to share what questions they believe their strategy should answer. There is no such thing as a bad question. Encourage people to dig deep. Ask people to write their questions down on cards and then cluster and headline them. It is easy to then compare these questions with your existing strategy and to make adjustments where needed. It brings people closer to the strategy, creates clarity and encourages higher levels of collaboration.

Uncertainty Mapping

Ask the leadership team, or again a larger audience of leaders to share everything that is uncertain or unclear about your strategy. Encourage people to clear their minds and their hearts of uncertainty and bring it into the room. You can ask people to write on cards, clustering them and then you can map the various themes. While you cannot promise to remove all of the uncertainly from the strategy, you do create a process for managing uncertainty. Topics can be assigned to various groups, who can work on them and report back at future sessions. This exercise helps people take ownership of their strategy and gives them a constructive way to deal with issues that might be slowing down strategic execution.

Framework and Flow

You may have heard the phrase, *they cannot see the forest for the trees,* meaning that someone is so consumed with details that they miss the big picture, let us say the overall strategic flow. When this happens in strategy work, it is difficult to own something that you have lost sight of.

Ask the leadership team (with teams larger than six you can build two groups) to simply diagram or visualize how strategy works in your organization. What are the top five strategic priorities and which functions contribute to which priorities? How does communication and collaboration work? How does top down and bottom up communication really flow? How do functions interact to take decisions, share resources and manage trade-offs in your business?

This sounds like a simple task, yet I have seen dozens of senior executives surprised by the ways their management team sees the strategic process working in their company. Again, calibrating expectations and making sure that everyone is on the same page leads to deeper ownership by all.

Our strategy is too complex; it is a strategy on paper,

but not something we or our people can practically carry forward.

A leadership team asked for my impressions of their new strategy. Their goal was to create more traction (aligned focus with collaborated action for results) with a new strategy in their organization. The document was 90 pages long. Well written, but far too much material for anybody to carry forward.

"Imagine this leadership team has to walk through the desert," I said. "How much water do you need to take with you?"

"As much water as we can", someone replied.

"What would happen, if you were trying to pull a two ton trailer full of water across the desert, with only the people power in this team," I asked.

"We would never be able to pull a load like that. We would all die in the desert," another team member replied.

If you want to hold water, you need a container. Strategy is no different. Yet if your container becomes too big, or too complex; people will not be able to wrap their arms, nor their imagination around it.

In the situation just mentioned, a meaningful discussion took place and the leadership team agreed that to help people connect to the strategy meant that everyone should be able to carry it, at least their part. Redesigning the "strategic container" helped people throughout the organization understand the whole and carry their part. While business plan reviews require deep back-ups, risk analysis overlays and, at times future scenarios, leadership teams must be conscious about how much strategy they expect people to carry. Certainly no more that they and their people can carry.

There is a feeling in our team that

not everyone is really on board with our strategy.

These are statements that you would normally not let to pass, without calling on the leader to be more specific. The person speaking is not speaking in the first person and they are not being specific.

Sometimes I will let such a statement pass through, especially if I see other executives passively agreeing with it, as it could be the right time to make things physical and put your strategy on the ropes. It works like this:

Clear the chairs and lay out a ten-meter rope on the floor, that is a bit over 30 feet so you need a good sized room for this. Label the "top end" of the rope, **Rationally Clear** and label the other end of the rope, **Not Rationally Clear**. Explain that this y-axis rope is how rationally clear each member in the leadership team thinks the current strategy is. It is important to point out to people that there are no good, bad, right, or wrong responses, rather a way to find out how clear the strategy is by each member the team.

Before people start to move to one end of the rope or the other, take another ten-meter rope and lay it perpendicular to the first rope. This is your x-axis rope and now the two ropes intersect in the middle and it looks like a cross or four quadrants without a border around them. On the x-axis rope, label the left side **Not Emotionally Connected** and on the right side, label this end, **Highly Emotionally Connected**. The ropes of the floor look like Fig. 7.1:

Now ask people to go and stand somewhere in the quadrants that expresses how rationally clear they find the strategy and how emotionally connected they feel the strategy is for them. Taking a personal stand and putting your strategy on the ropes, so to speak, with your leadership team is really an eye opener.

It is important that people do not judge others by where they stand. Everyone has the opportunity to share why they chose to stand where they did. This is a constructive exchange for the team and can be followed up with ideas to help everyone move to the upper right hand quadrant, the fertile field of high performance.

This activity can also be done on a flip chart and people can make their "personal stand" with a dot in the process visual, however physically standing and declaring why you chose that spot, and hearing the statements from everyone in the leadership team can become a pivotal moment for renewed ownership.

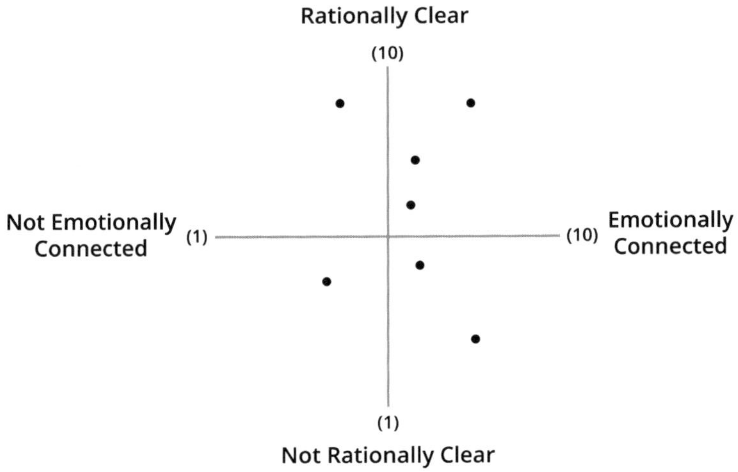

Fig. 7.1 Strategy on the ropes

> Our overall strategy, the big points are clear, but we don't understand the priorities of functions outside our own. We have "silent wars" and compete against, instead of compliment, each other.

Ownership extends beyond one's business function. Senseful strategy means leaders look beyond their functional boundaries to understand what peer leaders are out to accomplish and explore ways to help them be successful. In the language of executive ownershift, ownership means to the overall strategic priorities for the business. This means that every leader in the business must be deeply involved with their priorities and at least the priorities of the business one level above them. These can only be fulfilled through meaningful and efficient collaboration between the functions, a core practice of highly effective leadership teams.

Organizational charts and process flows indicate how things should work, but in reality they do not work automatically because collaboration and working together are strongly influenced by people and the situation at hand.

Regular expectation exchanges between leaders (and their functions) help people calibrate how their work influences and supports speed and growth with different parts of the business. This enables leaders to learn from other peer leaders and other functions how well (or not) they help others to be successful.

In short, each leader does some preparatory work; to share how they experience the business collaboration between different leaders in the team and the functions they represent.

Imagine you have a leadership team with eight members, including the CEO. Each member of the team gets a blank matrix that looks like this. In this case, this would be what the CEO's sheet looks like:

Business function	"What I'd like to see your function continue doing as it strengthens our collaboration"	"What I'd like to see your function start doing that would make our collaboration more effective"	"What I'd like to see your function stop doing that would make our collaboration more effective"
CEO			
Finance			
Human resources			
Legal and compliance			
Marketing			
Manufacturing			
Sales			
Supply chain			

Each function leader puts him or herself at the top of the matrix, spending a few minutes to identify some feedback points for each of their colleagues. A well-structured expectations exchange that brings a deeper understanding of how functional leaders support each other towards collective ownership of the overall business strategy.

This leadership team would then break into four pairs, each person in the pair shares their view with the leader they are sitting with, (three other pairs are doing the same) and after ten minutes, everyone finds a new partner. During the ten minutes, both leaders will share their insights with each other. This process repeats itself until each leader has had seven conversations. Leaders take a week or two to reflect on the feedback they have gotten and come back with renewed commitments to practice higher levels of collaborative excellence, which then becomes the new standard to cascade through the organizations.

Often executive leaders tell me it is one of the most helpful activities that they have ever done as a leadership team. It is simple, effective and easy to use at other levels of your organization.

> We are not good at prioritizing, everything is important.
>
> We don't dare close down projects.

It is impossible to create and maintain high levels of strategic ownership, over long periods of time when people do not believe the mission is worthy or achievable. Leadership teams that allow too many priorities to seep into their strategy can inflict serious damage to an ownership culture. Meaningful contributions diminish, because everyone has to spread their contributions across so many "so called priorities" that nothing really moves.

Senseful strategy means selecting initiatives that enable the company to succeed, and in most instances, leadership teams are never short of ideas of what could be added to bring more results to their strategic efforts. Yet when I challenge teams about what they intend to stop doing; the projects, programs and initiatives will they abandon in order to support the new initiatives they want to start, the room becomes silent. Letting go, abandoning or strategically quitting, as friend and performance guru Paul Rulkens would say, is difficult, however essential, to ensure that strategy is effective [3].

Leader teams that work with me vigilantly map priorities to ensure that their organization does not drown in the waters of "everything is important." You know the place, where everything is a priority, and when this happens, nothing is a priority. Without regular priority mapping, projects back up, resource wars start and results suffer. Priority mapping should cascade through the organization to ensure that things stay lean.

> People miss deadlines, projects are delayed and our product launches do not go as planned. Nothing happens. We don't have a culture of consequences here.

In a senseful strategy, you find a culture of consequences. Superficial strategy is heavy with "front-end load," characterized by excessive communication about what should be done, with light or little back-end follow up, feedback or consequences. Front-end information is helpful and necessary to let people know what needs to be done, but it is a poor way to encourage new behaviors (always required in a senseful strategy that is about improvement and growth) or to correct or modify behaviors that do not contribute to strategic targets.

Aubrey Daniels (Bringing Out the Best in People) has well-written books that are helpful resources to consequence cultural building [4].

In short, Daniels shares that the most effective consequences to encourage new behaviors are positive, immediate and certain. Let us call them PIC consequences. People do what they do largely because of the consequences they get for their behaviors. If you find yourself growing frustrated because things do not happen as you expect, stop repeating your messages and start looking at the consequences people get. There lies the clues to behavioral change.

All too often I am asked to speak to a promising executive who "has the right stuff" but has one or more destructive behaviors that is making it difficult for others to follow them and play at their best. The executive's boss and head of HR will describe how this person's behavior is putting that person's career at risk as well as their business.

I ask to see the leader-in-question's "song sheets," that is their previous performance appraisals or simply ask how long the executive in question has been aware of their destructive behaviors. After an uncomfortable silence, someone will say, "Well, this stuff is sort of written between the lines – we're not really sure that he or she is aware of how potentially negative these behaviors are." It is no wonder that people continue to do what they do, when consequences are not present.

When leaders observe behaviors that contribute to a senseful strategy, positive consequences (recognition, praise, remuneration) should follow and when people (including leaders) behave in a way that heads down the superficial strategy path, consequences (feedback, critique or penalties) should come quickly so that people are clear what is expected of them.

It is important to remember that every company has a strategy. It is your organization's path to the future. How certain you and your leadership team sound the trumpet will steer people to the senseful strategy path or the superficial strategy path.

The choice is yours.

What are you waiting for? Sound your trumpets!

References

1. Nanninga, G. (1998). *The dance of strategic planning*. Morrisville, NC: Lulu Press.
2. Tregoe, B. B., & Zimmmerman, J. W. (1980). *Top management strategy, what it is and how to make it work*. New York: Simon & Schuster.
3. Rulkens, P. (2018). *How successful engineers become great business leaders*. New York: Business Expert Press LLC.
4. Daniels, A. (2013). *Bringing out the best in people, how to apply the astonishing power of positive reinforcement*. New York: McGraw-Hill Publishing.

8 Creating an Ownership Epidemic

Imagine what your company could do if a culture of ownership went viral in your organization.

8.1 It's Not My Dog

A man walks into the hotel lobby and the clerk checks him in. The guest sees a cute little dog near the reception desk and asks, "Does your dog bite?"

"No," replies the hotel clerk.

The guest bends down to pet the cute little dog and the dog nearly bites off the man's hand.

Frightened out of his wits and exasperated, the guest screams, "I thought you said your dog doesn't bite!"

The clerk looks up and nonchalantly says, "It's not my dog."

While this scene may be familiar and humorous, the story is a powerful reminder of what is at stake for leaders who struggle to create and lead organizations of highly engaged employees.

You may not have dogs biting customers in your company lobby, but how often in meetings, projects or in the hallways do you hear people say, in different ways: "It's not my dog."

"It's not my dog" is another way of saying, I do my job, do what I am responsible for. You can even hold me accountable to additional tasks, but that is all that I am paid to do so that is what you get.

The costs associated with, "It's not my dog," are staggering. It is the terrible (and avoidable) cost of poor employee engagement. The Gallup Organization recently reported that poor employee engagement costs industry $500 billion dollars a year, in the USA alone [1].

Let me share another story, this one more personal and closer to home.

D. Norenberg, *Executive Ownershift*, Management for Professionals,
https://doi.org/10.1007/978-3-030-35828-0_8

8.2 Boomer

My sister was a softball player, and a good one at that. She played in youth leagues, junior high and high school and then, after receiving an athletic scholarship, played at the University of Northern Iowa, winning the national championship, her freshman year.

After spending one summer holiday with me in Redondo Beach, near Los Angeles, she decided that three years of Iowa winters were enough, and chose to finish her academic studies and her softball career, playing for the San Diego State Aztecs.

Los Angeles is only 2 h from San Diego. It was easy for me to drive down to San Diego and watch my little sister play softball with some of the best players in the United States.

At dinner one night, I asked, "How's your game going?"

"Overall, pretty good," she replied.

She had sticky hands, meaning she could catch any ball that came her way. She had an arm like a cannon and could throw as strong as any man I knew.

"So, what is the weakest part of your game?" I asked.

"It's my hitting, I am just not consistently hitting the ball like I know I can," she said.

We talked about this part of her game, her weak link as she called it. A few days later, Laura called me, thanked me for dinner and our conversation. She told me that she had asked another girl to come to practice an hour early and pitch to her. She wanted to get some extra time at bat, to work on her hitting consistency.

That is my sister, not satisfied with her fantastic ball handling skills, or throwing; instead picking out the weakest part of her game and investing extra time to improve it.

This story does not stop here. As my sister told me later, after about a week of her and another girl coming to practice early, another player asked if she could join them before practice as well, for some additional batting practice.

A week later, two other girls joined them and within three weeks, the entire team was showing up to practice and games early, in order to get an extra hour to improve their game.

My sister's hitting consistency improved. The head coach and other players started to call her Boomer, to describe the way she hit the ball. Not only did my sister's game get better, so did the performance of many players. Most surprising, my sister said, was the unexpected improvement in the team spirit and collaboration. This came, she said, through the extra time that each player volunteered, for themselves, and for team.

The "Boomer Epidemic," sparked by my sister's desire to improve, touched other players on the team that led to improved team performance and a highly positive and engaging team spirit. All of this took place without the intervention, orders or suggestions from the coach staff.

These two stories shape the context for a leadership team's greatest challenge. How does a leadership team do everything possible to ensure that people are highly engaged and play at their best?

8.3 Three Levels of Engagement

The hotel lobby scene outlines the three levels of engagement. The clerk did his job. He checked the guest in. He was responsible. We can even presume that he is accountable for the petty cash box under the register. Yet, we see that the clerk did not own the customer experience or he never would have let a guest bend down and meet a small dog with a big bite.

My sister and her softball colleagues understood their team responsibilities and were accountable for their individual team roles. Their efforts did not stop there, however. They chose, one by one and then collectively to go beyond what was asked of them. There was no coach standing over their shoulder, suggesting, directing or ordering those women to show up early. It was a choice made by one (my sister) that was replicated by the rest of the team members. The voluntary expression to do more, to give more, to create beyond what is prescribed or delegated to us, marks the ownership space, the third and highest level of engagement. Figure 8.1 illustrates the three levels of engagement and business impact:

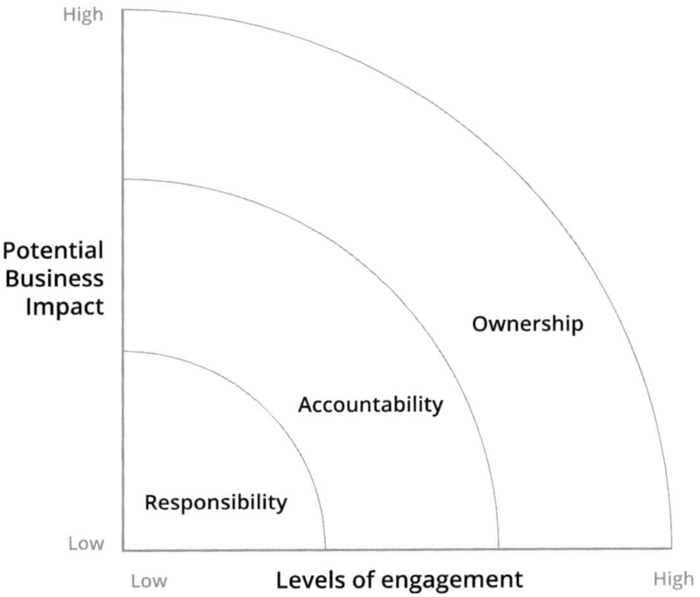

Fig. 8.1 Engagement impact map

Start with responsibility. This is the first level of engagement. You understand and do what is asked of you. Responsibility leads to clarity, an important component of engagement. Responsibility can be collective, such as sharing the responsibility for safety in a production facility. As a leader, I can delegate responsibility.

Accountability is similar to responsibility, as it can be delegated. Yet accountability is different from responsibility because it cannot be collectively distributed. It belongs to one person. A petty cash box is a simple example. Only one person can be accountable for the petty cash balance, so only one person has access or a set of keys to the petty cash box.

Now to ownership. People choose to take ownership for something. Ownership leads to the highest levels of engagement and business impact. Leaders sometimes say, "I need to delegate more ownership," and I remind them that this is not possible. What leaders can do is to create an environment that invites people to take ownership, yet it is the "I choose to commit to this" attitude that encourages discretionary efforts, the gold standard of engagement. This is why ownership is so highly desired, because when someone takes ownership, people exercise the highest level of engagement.

From my experience, responsibility gets you in the game, accountability helps you win the game and ownership enables you to dominate the game.

8.4 The Leadership Team Incubator

The word epidemic often describes a problem that has grown out of control. Medical professionals describe an epidemic as the rapid and widespread occurrence of an infectious disease, to a large number of people, within a certain area over a particular time.

Tuberculosis, malaria, influenza, and the Ebola virus are examples of modern day epidemics. The bubonic plague (the Black Death), yellow fever and small pox were other disease driven epidemics that wiped out large populations over our history.

Yet there is another side to this word epidemic. Working with organizations on three continents the past twenty years, I have seen change and improvement accelerate through positive and rapid transformation. Let me call these transformations positive epidemics, and from my experience, they are characterized by high levels of engagement, a collective willingness to unselfishly collaborate and a radical desire to challenge the status quo.

Researchers have confirmed that there are indeed, positive epidemics, as reported by Elizabeth Anderson, in the Parent Herald. The Sante Fe Institute, in New Mexico, USA, has studied positive epidemics for years, which can spread quickly, according to their research [2].

The Santa Fe Institute, ranked as one of the world's top 20 science and technology think tanks, has done groundbreaking work in this area. They defined the unit of transmission in positive (beneficial) epidemics. They call this unit of transmission a bene, which could be an idea, a technology, or a behavior—

something that offers an advantage and can spread through a population. According to the Santa Fe Group, positive (social) epidemics are transmitted by active spreading strategies of the people involved. Additionally, Benes have two hallmark traits: they are transmitted horizontally and offer some benefit to their host.

We know that environmental factors influence disease driven epidemics. These factors include water supply, sanitation behavior and facilities, food as well as climate.

Social epidemics are no different. Environmental factors also influence the degree that positive epidemics can take off, in your organization, for example.

The executive team is the most significant environmental influencer in your organization.

Why?

Setting strategic direction, allocating resources, developing compensation systems and decision-making all take place in the executive team. This is the birthplace of your organizational culture. The leadership team is the incubator for social epidemics in the organization. Executive teams can have a positive effect (like Boomer) or it operates in such a way that it transmits mistrust, fosters a competitive instead of a collaborative climate or leads with a superficial view of what the customer means to the business.

Executive leaders do not knowingly sow seeds of mistrust, drive unhealthy competition or belittle customers. Yet these "negative epidemics" do take hold in companies where leadership talk does not match leadership walk. Leaders underestimate how small inconsistencies in their team communication and collaboration are magnified and cascade through the organization.

An executive leader rarely says, I do not trust another member of my executive team, yet his or her actions will give people evidence (from what they observe and hear) needed to make their own determination.

As executives develop a deeper understanding (and respect) for the environmental influence that their leadership team has on the whole business, they ask the following questions:

What would an ownership epidemic mean to our business?
What could be the basis or foundation of such an epidemic in our organization?
How can we create the conditions for positive epidemics to take place, to encourage and invite people to join us in the ownership space?

8.5 Three Steps to Your Ownership Epidemic

Leadership teams can contribute to ownership epidemics in three ways:

(1) **Leadership teams must look at themselves candidly**; how they communicate, interact with each other and drive business strategy, from the point of view of others. How would a panel of customers feel if they were to sit in on

one of your board meetings? Do the people that report into the senior leadership team perceive this group as a cohesive and effective team, and if not, why? Do those around the leadership team sense that this group is open and ready to change themselves, or do they see this as the task of others?
Using an external advisor to observe management meetings or gather anonymous feedback from those reporting into the senior leadership team can help the team become more aware of how they can stimulate, rather than hinder, an ownership epidemic in the making.

(2) **Ownership epidemics are more than a head game**. Creating a compelling invitation for your employees to become part of an ownership culture means attracting people's heads, as well as their hearts. A voluntary shift into the ownership space involves a compelling mission, such as:

- **Uniting as one team, one company with one voice**. This drove the ownership culture at Ciba Vision (now Alcon), sponsored by Dietrich Fechner and Chris Olson. Iwis CEO Frank Wiemer also used one team, one voice as the through line in his organizational transformation.
- **Once in a lifetime opportunity. If not now, then when?** Jacques Richier, Allianz France CEO drew heavily on "a once in a lifetime opportunity" to motivate three highly successful, yet different businesses to come together as the newly created Allianz Worldwide Partners. Jacques continually reminded those around him that such opportunities, even in a large enterprise like Allianz, are rare and should and must be embraced by those executives presented with such an opportunity.
- **Putting the customer at the center of everything you do**. Dr. Lars Hendrikson, Dentsply Sirona Implants Vice President, realized that after two large mergers and business restructurings, his organization had turned their attention and energy inward, managing internal aspects of their business. He and his leadership realigned attention and energy to focus on their markets, and more specifically, putting the customer first and at the center of their ownership epidemic. You will hear more from these leaders and their experiences in Chap. 9, Executive Insights from the field.

(3) **Structure the space for the ownership invitation**. You cannot command, order or delegate people into the ownership space. High levels of engagement, fueled by a feeling of ownership, are a result of the choices that people make. Attempts to manipulate people into the ownership space is futile. We sometimes hear this after poor results of an engagement survey are shared across the company. Hints and even veiled threats such as, "you have to raise your engagement survey numbers" is a clear indication that executives have not really understood how they influence engagement in their organizations. Leaders can and will create more significant results when they strive to create the characteristics or markers of an ownership epidemic.

8.6 Nine Markers of the Ownership Epidemic

Outcome driven

People gravitate to the ownership space when people talk about outcomes and results; instead of long discussions, that seeks validation through activities alone.

Why is clear and present

Why questions and conversations trigger purpose and meaning, fundamental to ownership cultures.

Negotiations are part of agreements

In an ownership culture, you have the opportunity to discuss and negotiate agreements. If you expect others to simply do what they are told to do, with no opportunity to push back and challenge, you will not find people willing to join your ownership epidemic.

Emotionally present and engaging

The step into high engagement via ownership is more than an intellectual exercise. Emotionally present people speak with passion and conviction, connecting what they do and how they do it with shared values and purpose.

Recognition and rewards

Recognition and rewards are consistently used to acknowledge achievement in an ownership epidemic.

Shift orientation

Ownership epidemics are characterized by a "shift orientation", meaning that people are continually looking for ways to challenge the status quo, change and improve themselves and their business.

Honor the cause spirit prevails

Connecting with the goals and objectives beyond those that you personally control is honoring the cause spirit. Honor the cause spirit means putting the customer and your company ahead of personal or departmental issues. Leaders participating in the ownership epidemic are prepared, at times, to take decisions that may be good for the overall company, yet influence them or their business unit negatively.

Involvement breeds initiative

If a few executives at the top of the organization closely control decision-making, power and everything that shapes the business, you will not give birth to an ownership epidemic. Getting people involved through risk taking and decision making are key to an ownership culture. Involvement breeds commitment and encourages personal initiative.

Promise driven conversations prevail

Ownership epidemics are characterized by promise-driven conversations. Making and keeping promises strengthens commitments and builds trust throughout the organization.

8.7 Town Halls and Strategy Circles

Creating a culture of ownership is a process, rather than a one-time event. Saying that, there is often a starting point, a reset, a collective experience that can serve as a catalyst to quickly start and spread a positive epidemic of ownership.

This can take place through large group learning sessions, like interactive town hall sessions, strategic off-sites and strategy circles. These experiences go by different headlines; however, they often share similar characteristics:

- The leadership group size ranges from between 30 and 300, in addition to the executive team, all of which are present.
- Sessions take place off-site, away from the company and day-to-day operational distractions.
- They usually involve one or two overnight stays, enabling people to spend time together in informal settings, developing relationships and deepening their understanding of the day's content and challenge at hand.
- There is a strong call to action, often anchored in a larger than life opportunity, an overwhelming challenge or a disruption to core business activities and results.

Effective large group learning sessions, those that truly invite and support people to join the ownership space, work when three fundamental principles are in place:

1. **The executive team walks the talk**, demonstrating aligned conviction and action as they create, share and invite the next one or two leadership levels in their organization to embark on a journey with them.
2. **Such large group sessions are structured, yet the outcomes cannot be scripted beforehand**. Designing effective large group learning sessions means providing enough structure to guide the process, yet open enough to enable people to make choices, contribute and express both agreement and dissent. Executives that want to control off-sites through series of presentations (conference style) or avoid trending on sensitive subjects by insisting that "everyone stay positive" may ignore the emotional truths that could be released and acknowledged to reset the atmosphere and culture.
3. **Effective large group learning sessions work when there is strong energy, effort and resources to follow through on agreements**. Linking outcomes,

commitments and promises from large group sessions with consequences, helps channel large group enthusiasm into forward progress and tangible results.

Outside facilitators can help guide the process, enabling executives and other leaders present to be able to concentrate on the priorities at hand, but make no mistake about it, the heavy lifting, the backbone of these tipping point learning experiences rests with the executive team and other leaders present. Through the facilitation of hundreds of off-sites over the years, I have seen some remarkable experiences that led to sustainable ownership epidemics. These *ownershifting* experiences require work beforehand in the executive team, thereby deepening their conviction and resolve to their ownership epidemic.

Amer Ahmed, CEO of Allianz Reinsurance, encourages and supports large group learning experiences. He and his executive team conduct annual Strategy Circles, with 60 of their top leaders and talents every year. The Strategy Circle objectives include:

- Clarify the coming strategic priorities for the year and beyond.
- Work out a joint plan for collaboration excellence and execution.
- Work through the strategic priorities down through the functional team level.
- Acknowledge contributions from leaders and talents to the group's success.
- Clear up personal and functional blindspots through feedback exchanges.
- Ensure a high level of personal buy-in from those present to carry the strategic plans forward.

From my experience, large group learning experiences must be more than "information downloading", characterized by presentation after presentation. Results oriented large group learning session should address both business and human relationship topics in a balanced way. Sometimes, the organizers of such events try to over structure them and to eliminate uncertainty and take advantage of every minute that people are together. My clients create breakthroughs in the large group off-sites because they do not over structure them. Sessions are lightly structured to enable people to step forward, involve themselves and make something of the ideas and insights developed over the sessions.

Some sessions involve "all hands on deck," meaning everyone is together in one room; yet it is the breakout sessions and mixing people that ensures networking and relationship building takes place. This investment in networking and relationships pays forward towards a highly collaborative environment, a hallmark of ownership epidemics.

A senior R&D leader stood up recently at a strategic off-site, intended to reset the direction of the entire business, and said, "I've been with this company for thirteen years. Never in this time did the entire leadership team participate in an event with us from start to finish, and do so with such a visible alignment to one direction. This is tremendously motivating for me, and I believe I speak for many others here as well."

Money might buy love, but you cannot buy an ownership culture for your organization. To create deep levels of engagement in your business, insist that people have control over the outcomes they create. Help people throughout your organization see how the business is improving and be sure that folks who work in your company feel that their work is recognized and contributes to the overall growth of your business.

References

1. Gallup, Inc. (2013). *The State of the American Workplace: Employee Engagement Insights for U.S. Business Leaders*. Washington, D.C.: Gallup, Inc.
2. Anderson, E. (2016). *Positive epidemics' exist, spread faster than negative ones*. Los Angeles, CA: Parent Herald. https://www.parentherald.com/articles/40240/20160430/study-positive-epidemics-exist-spread-faster-negative-ones.htm.

Leading a Team of Leaders

9

None of us is as smart as all of us.

In the last three chapters, we explored how to make meetings matter (Chap. 6), the steps to build and lead a senseful strategy (Chap. 7) and the path to create an ownership epidemic in your organization (Chap. 8).

The leadership team shapes and anchors these cornerstones of high performance through the way they work together and interact with their organization. We know now what must go right as executives make choices (and sacrifices) to forge together as a true team of leaders, rather than a collection of soloists, committed only to their personal or functional success.

The journey to perform as a highly effective leadership team would not be complete without looking at the executives that head up these teams.

In every leadership team, there stands one person that encourages, guides and sometimes demands things from the team. How does one balance being a member of the leadership team and at the same time, as the head of this team, challenge and stimulate them to move beyond their comfort zone? How does the leader hold team colleagues accountable when one deviates from agreed norms? How, as the most senior executive, do you decide which of the many initiatives to choose from, that will steer the company successfully into the future?

Literature even today continues to spotlight the heroic leader, an *extraordinaire* individualist, as the "saving grace," for many a team or company's success. Experienced executives today know better. It is easy to shine the light on one person, and say they made it all possible, but this would only be fitting for a Hollywood script and not truthfully explain how real leadership teams succeed. Michael Jordan, the legendary basketball superstar, was heard to have said, "Talent wins games, but teamwork wins championships."

Renowned leadership coach Marshall Goldsmith says this about leading teams of leaders:

D. Norenberg, *Executive Ownershift*, Management for Professionals,
https://doi.org/10.1007/978-3-030-35828-0_9

> It is not realistic to expect any one individual to possess all the various iterations of strengths and skills necessary to lead a company through a decade or more of roller coaster markets, global expansion and economic changes…the global leader of the future should concentrate on building a team of leaders who (1) feel a sense of ownership for the business, and (2) can rely on each other's strengths during different challenges the company will face [1].

Unfortunately, Michael Jordan, Marshall Goldsmith, or any executive that leads teams of leaders, cannot give us a simple checklist to make all of the above happen. We can accelerate the speed at which we adapt, grow and ultimately perform by listening, *and learning*, from executive experiences, reflecting on their struggles, and their successes.

Some of the deepest insights about life, leadership and teamwork come during after-hour exchanges, fireside chats and small, intimate settings where leaders speak candidly about their concerns, frustrations, and aspirations. Executives often say that when they look back at their team transformation process, the fireside chats, with its non-judgmental atmosphere, were team-tipping points for them.

With this in mind, I invited six executives to share their experiences and wisdom. They come from a variety of industries and different cultural backgrounds. Each of them asked me at some point to support their executive team growth process and at that time, each led a business or company that was doing business across the globe. (I have described their business and their role as it was when we worked together.)

They are very successful leaders yet in no way do I want to describe them as perfect, or always getting it right. Nevertheless, their approach to business, their intention to create a true team of leaders, and most importantly, their willingness to share their vulnerabilities and own their challenges as the starting point for team and organizational change is executive courage in action, and therefore worthy of our attention.

9.1 Fireside Wisdom Exchange

To make the most of our experience exchange, imagine that we are sitting comfortably with these executives, around the fireplace, wonderfully warm, intimate and inclusive. The atmosphere is open and inviting, everyone is willing to share, and eager to listen and learn from the experiences of the others.

As you listen to the wisdom shared by these executives, reflect on their experiences and how they address the following questions and what these insights could mean for you:

- What are the "must haves" for an executive team to play at their best?
- How have you managed and come through tough challenges?
- What is important when stepping into an executive team role?

9.2 Ervin Appelfeld, Global Head of Manufacturing, ZF

Results through respect

ZF is a leader in automotive driveline and chassis technology as well as active and passive safety technology, with a global workforce of 146,000 at approximately 230 locations in some 40 countries. With annual sales of nearly €40 billion, it is one of the largest automotive suppliers in the world.

Ervin is the head of global production, responsible for 20,000 people spread over 45 production sites. He is originally from the Czech Republic and is now based in Koblenz, Germany. Here are Ervin's insights:

> It is not the machines, technology or the processes that makes you successful. At the end of the day, the deciding factors to your success are people, the behaviors they practice and the culture that you (and the team) create so people can perform.
>
> This is the message that I consistently share with leaders and people throughout our organization.
>
> Our success resides in our people and this comes down to respect. If people respect me, they will follow my leadership. If I respect others, it allows me to develop deeper relationships with them. This is core to the success of any leadership team.
>
> When you respect someone's strengths, and their needs, you form stronger, more trusting relationships with them.
>
> In the German culture, where I am based, business and private life is separated. I tell my people, if you want to keep your private life separate, that is fine and I will respect that. When you do share with me what is going on in your life, what is running in the background or when you have troubles; I can support you in deeper ways.
>
> For example, sometimes you sense it is time to come down hard on something or somebody, and you do so without knowledge that something is running wrong in their private life; it might get even more complicated.
>
> Here is my advice for newly appointed executives:
>
> – Do not take decisions because you do not like something.
>
> – Make decisions that support your aspirations and what is good for the business.
>
> – I do not like negatively driven decisions - they always come back and make your life, and your business, more complicated.
>
> – Do not be afraid to use outside help, I have used outside consultants over the years, especially when it involves a lot of change or team redesign and this has been very valuable for us.

When I asked Ervin what was helpful or valuable about my contributions to his leadership team growth process he said,

> Getting leaders to run their function and be a valuable member of the senior leadership team involves a lot of give and take, making adjustments and, at times, compromising. You continually adjusted the off-site agendas to address the issues that were essential to us. This was very helpful and a good example of how we needed to work with each other to manage

the different agendas that all of us bring into the senior leadership team. Be prepared to compromise and listen behind the words – often we say things differently but mean the same thing. You were an example to the team of how we could work together, in a fluid way with less rigidity.

9.3 Amer Ahmed, CEO, Allianz Reinsurance

People make the difference

Allianz Re is the reinsurance arm of the Allianz Group, a global financial services provider with services predominantly in the insurance and asset management business.

Allianz Re, with its headquarters in Munich, Germany, provides reinsurance solutions for the diverse business needs of their global customers. Amer has led this business since 2007, and during this period, he and his team of 550 professionals have grown the premium business from 4 to 6.6 billion euros, with annual profits of €500 million.

Amer reflected on his experiences and lessons learned as an executive leader.

I have always worked where significant change was required and I enjoy working through and improving situations where there is a lot of uncertainty. I come from a strong technical background, and my focus, in the past and even now, is on facts, figures and objective information.

One of my learnings, that I continue to work on today, is the importance of the human side of change and the time it takes to address the emotional issues. When you are at the top of an organization, it is easy to drive change, and understand it intellectually, and it is another thing to be confronted with a change process that you did not initiate.

We are in the reinsurance business. On one hand, our business is strongly influenced by facts and figures, yet through countless examples, I have learned how important it is to really involve people in this process. Often we get it right and sometimes we do not, and this continues to be a personal area of development for me, and my leadership team.

My advice for upcoming executives is to make certain that you continually inform, engage, and debate with your people so that they feel included. You can make all the right business moves, but if the people have not been brought along, you will not achieve what is truly possible.

Being an effective executive means learning to let go and trusting others to run with things. I still love diving deep in the details of the many exciting new things we bring to our clients, but I am learning to accept that listening to others and trusting their judgement is really the only way an effective executive can operate. This means spending more time and effort talking about why something is important versus how to do it.

Leadership teams can consume all of their time and energy discussing functional aspects of the business, (that is how things work), and company objectives, (the results we create), yet all high performing leadership teams, in my opinion, must invest time to discuss the purpose and role of what they do. When you do this at the leadership team level you can encourage these discussions at all levels of your business, but it has to start at the top.

People are the single most important part of our business, and I believe this is the case for most businesses, so it is essential that you pay attention and hire the best people you can get, for every position in the business. After they are on board, the real work starts and you have to invest in people or you will find yourself short of bench strength when you need it.

9.4 Dietrich Fechner, Managing Director, Ciba Vision Germany

Humble in the jungle creates relationships for results

CIBA VISION, now known as Alcon Vision Care, produces high quality contact lenses for daily and extended wear. The CIBA VISION DAILIES business segment involves 2,500 employees, manufacturing about 2.5 billion contact lenses annually and revenues of an estimated USD1 billion.

Dietrich led a group of pooled production sites in the US, Singapore and Germany as well as a large pan-European logistics organization. For more than 15 years he also led the largest and most advanced European manufacturing and R&D site in a highly regulated medical device field.

Dietrich shared his insights about creating buy-into a common agenda, one that is more comprehensive than simply a local agenda.

As CIBA Vision's Managing Director of Europe's largest contact lens manufacturing site located in Germany, I additionally was charged with the leadership role for all daily disposable contact lens manufacturing of CIBA Vision. This role involved plants in Atlanta, Georgia and Singapore.

All the plants were using the very same technology platform and all had the capacity to produce all variants of DAILIES. This setting required very close technical cooperation, mutual day-to-day support and accumulation of joint development projects for the greater good of global operation.

However, the three plants were also competitors. Their HC, TPC and quality data were easily comparable. Based on this data and performance, allocation of capital, cost budgets and product portfolio were determined.

The individual plant interests led to conflicts, some personal but more so due to cultural misunderstandings and the great distances and different times zones that people worked. Conflicts were present, yet each site had technical challenges that required the support of another site. My challenge and our business opportunity was to reconcile these adverse interests and to have all players volunteer for the greater good. I decided to conduct "Cultural Trainings" to bring together and bond the 25 top leaders of the three plants with Asian, American and German backgrounds.

Over the course of three years, we met for about a week each year in typical settings for each of the three regions: in a most basic Malaysian rain forest resort, a homespun Appalachian farmhouse and in an unpretentious German hunting lodge.

The simple and inexpensive settings served multiple purposes: leaders were asked to be humble and to focus on the essentials, they lacked any fancy distraction, thus fostering the get-together.

These daily training sessions aimed to generate cultural knowledge and understanding as well as friendship amongst the leaders. Business topics also came on the table, with the intention of putting ourselves in the other's shoes, looking to understand how other people operated and learning to develop common ground. The leisure time in morning and evening was not more (or less) than talking, bonding, having good times together.

Our cultural trainings garnered outstanding results: based on friendship and understanding the collaboration amongst the plants became a matter of daily course and the imminent competition turned into a healthy, constructive and collective battle for the greater good.

9.5 Jacques Richier, CEO, Allianz France

Listen, listen, listen, and then propose

Allianz provides insurance, assistance and financial services for individuals, professionals, businesses and communities, operating in more than 70 countries, with nearly 140,000 employees worldwide.

Jacques is the CEO of Allianz France, a multi-line insurer, specialists in wealth and social protection. He leads 9000 employees, with annual revenues of €12 billion and almost six million customers. He is based in Paris, France.

To be successful, diversity is key in an executive team in terms of profiles, characters and backgrounds. It is obvious that the entire team needs to share the same ambitions, methods and goals, but each one with their own perspective. Team members must feel free to speak frankly with the others, with consideration to their colleagues. In addition, the lower politics, the better.

One of my toughest challenges was when I became CEO of a large company, with more than 10,000 employees. I came from outside the company, whereas the tradition was to promote executives internally. Initially, coming from the outside was not an advantage. To succeed in such a situation, it was necessary to gain the acceptance of executives and to get support from managers who were recognized as 'transformers' or 'opinion leaders.' To build a highly effective executive team, it is essential that these executives share the same ambitions.

For a first executive team role, I would advise the following: listen, listen, listen, and then make proposals!

Another insight that has served me well: Consistency. Consistency is key in an executive team role. It is important to keep the consistency of the strategy and to explain it. You also have to be consistent regarding people issues, when it comes to promoting or dismissing someone – decisions have to be undisputable and exemplary.

9.6 Frank Wiemer, CEO, iwis motorsysteme

Think of yourself as an orchestrator, helping a talented team do what it does best

iwis motorsysteme manufactures high quality, precision chains for the automotive industry, with production facilities in Germany, China and the USA, through nearly

1,000 employees worldwide. iwis motorsysteme is part of the iwis Group, a fourth generation family business that specializes in high performance chain technology, headquartered in Munich, Germany. Frank is the CEO of iwis motosysteme and here are his reflections:

> Trust is the ingredient that moves good teams to great teams. Trust means the team members accept each other as responsible and competent to manage their particular function. When people start questioning each other's competence, you start to fail. The overall leader has to ensure that the right players are in the right positions.
>
> This was a big shift for us when Dan came in and started working with our leadership team. The quality of our questions is different now. Blaming is gone and our questions are more process driven and less about personal attacks. The trustful way of working and talking with each other has been institutionalized in our leadership team – and it moves to the other levels too.
>
> You do your best, but everyone at one point or another has hired the wrong person for a particular job. I have gotten personal feedback over the years that sometimes I wait too long to let the wrong person go. People get a year with me, and if I see that something is not working, I step in and see how I can help this person develop, to step up their game so they can play in the team. I am not a fan of letting people go too soon, before you have tried to help them make needed changes. When I do have to let someone go, I feel like I have failed.
>
> One of the things that is important to our future success is becoming more diverse. We are successful, yet very German, more than that, very Bavarian, and to continue to grow it is important that we develop a more inclusive culture.
>
> My advice for someone stepping into an executive role is simple. It is something my grandmother constantly shared with me: Treat people the way you want to be treated. This sounds so easy, but people do not always behave this way. I am conscious of my "grandmother rule" and think about this before I take major actions. I believe we meet people twice in life so this is a good rule to keep in mind and I just feel better when I act this way. I have tried to raise my kids this way as well.
>
> There are always pros and cons when you think about being a very strong, authoritarian type leader (a dictator for lack of a better word) versus building a well-balanced team of contributors.
>
> Yet authoritarian, dictator-driven structures have no sounding board to consider diverse ideas or changes in markets and at some point, all dictators fail. I much prefer working and leading a team of leaders. Certainly discussing issues takes more time, but a balanced team can help any senior leader, no matter how good they are, to cover for weaknesses that they have. We all have weaknesses and this is how a good team compensates. I would rather be seen as an orchestrator, helping a talented team learn who does what best and then how to support each other through the different challenges that come up through the business cycle.
>
> I grew up in Eastern Germany, part of the Soviet Bloc. While some might think this was a dictator driven society, I did not have that experience growing up. For me, it was teamwork in action. Our family had a farm, so we had a variety of ways to create food. Things we could not get, electrical wiring, tiles for the bathroom, or spare parts for the car, you had to go out and trade food that you had grown or raised for something that you needed. We were constantly negotiating and in most cases, trying to create win-win solutions. It was very

different in the West. In the West, money would get you what you need, in the East; money did not have nearly as much influence.

The take aways working with you, Dan, were that you helped us create deep levels of trust between each of us and as an entire team. This was very different from how we had been working previously. We got to know each other better, learned how we ticked, and this helped us understand each other's behaviors much better.

The second big take away were the tools and system for success you shared with us. Simple and effective. The result was that we are able to use these tools and frameworks throughout the organization. It is interesting to watch them move down through the different teams, helping people solve problems and giving us a common approach to dealing with our challenges.

9.7 Lars Henrikson, Group Vice President, Implants, Dentsply Sirona

Each of us sets the example for the change we expect in others

Dentsply Sirona is a global provider of professional dental products and technologies. Lars was Group Vice President of the Implant Group, with 2,400 people operating in 27 countries and revenues of $550 million. Lars shared the following insights:

Family is for me the most important thing in life and without this strong foundation, I could not have done the professional career that I have experienced. Also in my professional life, I have had a lot of luck. I have happened to be at the right place at the right time and thereby been given many opportunities when I was very young and an inexperienced leader.

I also have had the pleasure to work within the medical device industry, which means that you help people improve their quality of life. On top of all this, during my first 25 years as a leader (almost the whole time as part of the leadership team), the companies I worked for nearly always produced double-digit annual growth and gained market share year after year.

In these companies, we had a very strong customer focus and worked closely with our key customers, continually developing our products and services.

In the early days, we could sell our products based on product features and benefits but over time the products became more and more alike and service and support to the customers became a key differentiator.

To work in a company that grows every year and continually gains market share creates a positive corporate climate. You have of course challenges and obstacles to overcome, but with a strong momentum in the business, these are normally not too hard to handle.

I am, as a person, positive and optimistic. With the combination of my personality and the strong business momentum we had, our record of accomplishment was very good and I believed I was a good and strong leader during this time.

Things changed when a large global player acquired the company I worked for and within this global group, they merged my company with one of our major competitors, with the objective to become number one in the world.

18 months after the merger, I became the CEO, and during the time, our momentum and our growth stagnated. Before the merger we took growth for granted, now, after the merger, we were one company, but we still operated as two different company cultures. On top of all this, the mother company that owned us initiated a major reorganization of the whole group and we became very internally focused.

During my first year as CEO, I worked very hard and travelled around the world, first to communicate our new common values and strategies and try to convince my organization that the large restructuring of the group was going to be to our benefit even if I internally had, however, some doubts about the way forward.

I also was leading a new leadership team, one that I had more or less inherited because of the integration, 18 months earlier.

During this time, I slowly became more and more frustrated about how things were developing. Our topline had stopped growing, integrating two different corporate cultures proved to be extremely challenging, and on top of this we had become so internally focused that we had almost forgotten about our customers. I also felt that the way we worked in the leadership team was not what I was used to or what should be expected from a group that leads an organization of nearly 2,500 people.

I also realized at this time that my personnel frustration influenced me as a leader and that I was not as effective in my communication and interaction with my team as I used to be. This was a new experience for me; initially I did not know what to do. I was certain however, that I had to do something first about my own behavior, as well to create a more positive climate in our leadership team.

I have historically been skeptical about using external consultants, but this time I realized I needed someone coming from the outside, to help and support me and also work with my leadership team. Several members of my leadership team had worked with Dan in a European wide strategic leadership program and I invited Dan to support our executive team growth process.

I arranged a set of off-site meetings with my leadership team. The initial objectives were to get to know each other better as well as to create a strategy and story that truly could energize and engage the whole organization.

This first meeting was the starting point of a true turn around for me as a leader, and I regained my optimistic, energetic leadership style instead of being frustrated and negative. This led to a reset in the leadership team where we started to build a stronger, more resilient leadership team that could openly discuss and challenge each other, and finally agree on our way forward.

A key step in this process took place during the first off-site meeting with my team. Sitting in front of the fireplace, on the first evening, I opened up and told the team about my frustration, and how I felt bad about how I had worked as a leader during the last couple of months.

I believe my honesty and openness created the foundation for the others also to speak about their own feelings, concerns and frustrations.

From there on, we were able to slowly turn the situation around, creating one new corporate culture, and again getting the customer back in focus. In time, we slowly started to see our business grow again.

This took some time, but most important was that I was convinced we were now on the right track and my leadership team was onboard. This meant that we could show our ownership and alignment as a leadership team to the rest of the organization.

My key takeaways from this experience:

– To lead a growing and winning business can be very different to what it means to lead when things are not developing as strong.

– Be aware of how you, as a leader, react personally when things are not going exactly as you had hoped. You are still the one that people in the organization look to and they expect you to show them the way even if it is a tough road ahead.

– Be open and transparent with your team about challenges you see and how they can help you overcome these challenges as well as how you can help them.

– Never lose sight of your customers. It is so easy, especially when companies go through internal reorganizations, to become internally focused and forget about your customers. This gives your competitors an open door into your customers.

My final words: To work as a leader is in my experience extremely rewarding and one of the best things in life!

9.8 Executive Wisdom Consolidation

Ervin, Amer, Dietrich, Jacques, Frank and Lars lead executive teams in distinctly different industries and come from vastly different professional backgrounds. Their stories, however, are not told in isolation, but are part of a bigger picture. Through their lessons learned and my experiences of working with dozens of other senior leaders and their teams, we recognize behaviors and patterns that contribute to highly effective leadership teams and attitudes and actions that are counter-productive, which can sidetrack executive teams.

Leaders hinder teams when they fall into performance pitfalls and enable leadership teams when they use best practices. Let us look at performance pitfalls that leaders need to minimize or avoid and best practices to use generously with leadership teams.

9.9 Performance Pitfalls

When the senior leader does this, their team seldom plays at their best

(1) Insist on showing they are the smartest person in the room, and have the need to win every argument and take most if not all decisions in the leadership team
(2) Fail to admit their own shortcomings and how they contribute sub optimal performance, instead blaming someone or something else
(3) Hold individual team members accountable to personal and functional objectives, but fail to hold the team accountable for team or strategic priorities that could involve two or more members, thereby encouraging ownership for the overall team objectives

(4) Allowing the team to run down operational rabbit holes, distracting them from real executive teamwork and not staying true to purposeful, clearly defined strategic objectives
(5) Ignoring or not acting quickly and consequently when behavior issues fall outside of agreed upon norms or promises made in the team

9.10 Senior Leader Best Practices

When the senior leader does this, they help their team to play at their best

(1) Act upon the belief that their leadership team is the starting point and the tipping point for organizational change and renewed performance
(2) Able to express the challenge or poor performance present, coupled with their own authentic and emotional expressions of frustration, anger, not centered or blaming others, but taking ownership themselves
(3) Use outside expertise and consultants appropriately – not relying too heavily on outside consultants to do the job that the team should do, but rather using external expertise as a catalyst for change driven by the team
(4) Communicate a picture or vision of what future success could look like, with a compelling invitation for the team to influence, shape and construct how this future success comes to life. An equally important practice is the ability to convince others that the current status quo approach will not sustain or lead to a successful future
(5) Able to create an atmosphere where people feel safe, secure (yes, even at this senior level) and supported to stretch themselves, make mistakes and to show that they truly enjoy where they are and what they do

These best practices and performance pitfalls are not only for the senior leader in the team. These can and should be practiced by everyone in the leadership team. It is one of the huge benefits of executive ownershift. Everything that has been introduced can be replicated throughout the organization, creating a common language, common practices that lead to breakthrough results.

I have learned much from the six executives who shared their stories here. With an attitude and leadership approach that emphasizes success instead of perfection, they gain respect and attract like-minded professionals who value the same. With so many initiatives, challenges and surprises coming at them all the time, being able to learn from mistakes, focus on helping others succeed and being able to laugh at themselves from time to time are important ingredients for a leadership team brewing to play at its best.

Let us now move into Chap. 10 and review how you can make the most of your executive ownershift.

Reference

1. Hawkins, P. (2017). *Leadership team coaching, developing collective transformational leadership*. Great Britain and the United States: Kogan Page Publishing.

The Leadership Team 10

A sense of ownership is the most powerful weapon a team or organization can have.
— Pat Summitt

10.1 Prison Perspectives

I spent time in prison, a long time ago. Before you get nervous, let me explain. I studied psychology and criminology. As part of my criminology degree, I worked on a program called "Scared Straight" [1] with my professors.

We took young criminals (males between the ages of 18–24) into the Anamosa State Penitentiary, a maximum-security prison, located in eastern Iowa.

Criminal researchers and practitioners, at that time, believed that when young criminals saw what prison life was like, first hand, it would be so unpleasant that they would change their ways. Robbing small stores, stealing cars and carrying an unlicensed firearm were some of their offences.

It was a tough setting, six to eight prison inmates, sitting in a circle with me, my professor, and some not so seasoned, young criminals. In each corner of the room, an armed prison guard stood ready to neutralize situations that escalated. The older men (many of them in for life sentences) taunted the young criminals with a lot of profanity. They told these young men to change their ways before it was too late.

As profound as these experiences were, many of the men went back into the environments they came from. Back to an environment of drugs, violence, gangs and few of them had both parents at home. These young men returned quickly to their old habits. Their preexisting environment was stronger than their ability to change. Some of them were fortunate, however, and placed in new environments, with a distant relative, a trade school, or a foster home, away from their old neighborhood, old connections and old habits.

D. Norenberg, *Executive Ownershift*, Management for Professionals,
https://doi.org/10.1007/978-3-030-35828-0_10

Those who moved into new environments stayed out of trouble much more than the group that "returned home," to their original environments.

My Anamosa prison experience reinforces how futile individual change efforts are if the environment does not change.

Leadership development should and must take place as a team experience. We should not send a coached leader back into an uncoached team—this will not create large leadership returns or the desired organizational results.

Taking leaders out of their team and out of their environment for individual development is not the best way to improve leadership performance and will have little impact on your organization results.

We need to distinguish between **leader development**, that is support for an individual leader and **leadership development**, which involves the leader and her team. Individual leader development can support behavioral or skills issues for individuals, but only leadership development, as a team, can improve both leadership performance and organizational results.

Emphasis on leadership as a team endeavor is a competitive advantage over those organizations that continue to develop leaders as soloists, alone and separated from their teams where real organizational results are created. I believe that executive ownershift will become the driving force for leadership teams and organizations that play at their best.

How does **leader** development and **leadership** development work in your organization?

1. What percentage of your resources are committed to individual leader development compared to those resources allocated to leadership (team) development?
2. How many executive and strategic leadership teams do you have in your organization?
3. What system do you use to evaluate your leadership teams?
4. What process do the leadership teams you identified in question two use to share best practices and lessons learned with each other?
5. How do you share where leadership teams rank, from playing at their best to underperforming, with your respective leadership teams?
6. How regularly do you require leadership teams to self-evaluate and use first level reporting line evaluations to stimulate continuous improvement for every leadership team in your company?
7. How do you enable your leadership teams to play at their best?
8. How would your customers profit and what else would be different if your leadership teams played at their best?

10.2 Two Legged Stools Versus the IKEA Principle

What other remedies and approaches are available for executive and strategic leadership teams? Here are five approaches that are often used:

Business reviews or strategic reviews are standard practice for many leadership teams. In fact, I advise and observe many of these sessions. They help fine tune strategy and sharpen your strategic conversation; however, they are all too often mechanical, overly structured with too little space and time to discuss what is really blocking performance. Strategic reviews are often rolling forecasts, with growth plan projections based on past business assumptions that may or may not be relevant in the future. Often top down, tribunal driven, many leaders tell me they just want to "get done and get out;" missing the opportunity for deeper dialogs that could lead to business breakthroughs. Therefore, this remedy is helpful but not comprehensive.

Team building can go in many directions and while executive ownershift has a strong team development element; it has far more signature strengths. Team building often involves outdoor activities or an element of endurance or adventure. The value of such experiences depends less on the type of experience and more on the debriefing, reflection and learning transfer back into the team and the business. Team building is a nice to have, yet often fails to bring the critical business issues into discussion. Executive Ownershift does.

Personal coaching, life coaching and executive coaching are the cornerstones of many leader development programs. The introduction and use of coaching as it relates to leader development is a step in the right direction. The challenge with most personal coaching programs is that the coach and coachee work in isolation and far too few coaches actually observe the coachee putting into practice what was learned and agreed in the coaching sessions.

Institutional trainings involve learning rollouts to ensure that everyone has the same level of knowledge across the business. Often used for compliance or governance issues, a senior leader of a technology company told me that his leadership team (and all other leadership teams) were required to participate in a training program on emotional intelligence. When I asked how it was, he said, "What a waste of time". How unfortunate I thought, because emotional intelligence is a characteristic of high performance leaders and is a relevant theme for every leader. Yet it should not be packaged as "training," as executives do not see themselves in need of a training.

Business school excursions are attractive because people get out and get involved with professionals from other companies and industries. The challenge is that even the best of business school programs, when aimed at the individual level, fail to translate into tangible organization results.

The above-mentioned remedies bring some advantages and value to leaders and leadership teams, yet they could be compared to trying to sit on a two-legged stool; structured support to a degree, but not balanced enough that you can put your full weight into it.

Executive Ownershift provides balanced, comprehensive support to leadership teams. It is like the IKEA Principle. You put it together. Leaders that commit to an executive ownershift process build an executive agenda that clarifies the key areas that will move them and their team, learn to focus on those initiatives and commit to systematic follow through. It is a process that runs alongside of your business activities, addressing and improving real issues in real time, thus developing and improving a real leadership team.

Through my years of experience, I am yet to find a more meaningful and comprehensive way to grow both leadership performance and organization results than executive ownershift. Through its holistic, head and heart approach, I believe it brings the best of all worlds to the team and the organization they serve.

When to say no to Executive Ownershift

Does this mean that executive ownershift is right for every leadership team?

Of course not. There are the "no go markers" when screening and considering a leadership team for an executive ownershift intervention: If one or more of these markers in present, they must be discussed respectfully and directly with the senior leader of the team.

The six "no go" executive ownershift markers:

1. There is no respect between key players.
2. The top leader does not believe in taking ownership for their personal change or will not play.
3. There is a strong sense of entitlement, meaning, we are the top team, change and improvement should start anywhere but with us.
4. There is no sense of urgency, meaning the mindset of the team is stuck in denial or contentment regarding their team or their business.
5. Executives say, start at the lower levels, and work up.
6. There is no emotional competence or sensitivity within the team.

Four ways to eliminate "no go blockers" to your team's executive ownershift:

Mapping Our Journey of Untapped Potential—Visualize the distance from where they are today (as a business and a team) and where they could be if they were playing at their best.

Status Quo Balance Sheet—Consider the costs and risks, as a team and business, of the following question.

What does it cost for us to stay where we are?

(Use the tangible, intangible and peripheral cost framework described in Chap. 2 to explore the consequences of simply staying where you are).

Mirror Our Ways—What would happen if everyone in the company behaved and interacted the way that members of the senior leadership team behave and interact? This reflected discussion often opens the door to a readiness for personal and team change.

Outside Advisor Perspective—Ask the leadership team to imagine that they are an external consulting group looking at the business and the team. What advice do they have for the business, and particularly the team, that would increase effectiveness and results?

Taking ownership to a holistic approach to leadership team growth means working with the entire team, vigilantly sharing successes and lessons learned with other key leadership teams, and being sensitive to obstacles that prevent leadership teams from owning their own transformation as an example to others.

10.3 Put the Customer at the Center of Everything You Do

In Chap. 8, I introduced ways to stimulate an ownership epidemic that cascades out of the leadership team and into the organization. Let us return to this now and explore how to ensure the transformation that starts in your leadership team moves passionately throughout your company.

I have seen a number of ways that leadership teams instill a shared vision of their future success with their organization, yet none more powerful and sustaining than one that puts the customer at the center of everything you do.

Where and how is the customer positioned in your business?

What organizational language do you use to express where the customer stands with you?

- We are customer oriented.
- We are customer centric.
- The customer is king in our company.

This is weak language. It does not call people to action or ownership regarding the most important aspect of your business. Use this language and see how it feels:

We put the customer at the center of everything we do.

Now, how does that feel? Language like this shifts what you do and how you do it with the customer in the center. Many leaders talk about customer orientation, yet saying it is not doing it. Putting the customer at the center of everything you do means that people in your company physically meet and exchange with their customers. The benefits of these interactions include:

1. Get to know and make a connection with a select number of customers.
2. Develop a deeper understanding of customer motivations, aspirations and their perceptions of your company.
3. Learn what is working well for them and where they are struggling.

4. Collect ideas for deeper market analysis and validation.
5. Enable these select customers to feel appreciated and respected for their contributions to their industry and to your company's performance.

There are several ways that you can bring customers, and their experience into your organization, here is a format for customer exchanges, that has worked well for many of my clients. I have outlined the format, timing and potential questions for you.

Start with a short opening, perhaps by sharing something that changed the way you looked at things from an important customer experience and then introduce the customers briefly and share how the session will run, from a timing and structural point of view.

Allow each customer to introduce themselves in more detail, (ten minutes each) encouraging them to share why they got into this profession, something about their practice and what's important for them.

The lead person could start with a few questions to warm up the customers and audience, followed by a Q & A session with questions coming from the audience. The customers might have questions for the leadership team or the audience as well.

Customer Exchange Suggested Timing

(This format was used with three customers, as part of a larger leadership off-site with 80 people.)

Welcome and Intro	10 min
Personal Customer Intros	30 min
Q & A from Senior Lead	15 min
Group Q & A	60 min
Wrap Up and Consolidation	5 min

Possible introduction questions and impulses for the customers. (These should be sent in advance to offer some guidance about their personal introductions).

1. A personal introduction.
2. Your personal and professional pathway, areas of interest and/or expertise.
3. Unusual aspects about you or things people would not normally know about you.
4. Challenging situations in your career and how you overcame them and what you learned.
5. What is difficult for you as an industry professional today?
6. What you most enjoy about your work?
7. How you develop yourself as a professional?

Additional Questions

1. What do you think of this product or service?
2. What is the one thing we should do to make things better for you?
3. What should we stop doing?
4. Can you give me an example?
5. What annoys you about this product, about us, or our service the most?
6. How does or does not this product solve problem X for you?
7. What opportunities do you want to capitalize on or what problems would you most like to see us solve with you?
8. What are other providers/competitors offering, doing differently from us that you find attractive and valuable?
9. If you were to switch positions with our senior management, and you were in that role, what would you do and where would you focus your attention?

Considerations for Customer Exchanges

Use Why Questions to Follow Up

This is an insightful question and you can use it often. Do not simply accept a customer's first response and move on. By asking "why" as a follow-up question, you can often extract a more enlightening response and get to the crux of their issue.

How do you do that today?

This is a valuable question when a customer asks you for a specific feature. Rather than taking their feature request at face value, try to understand how they are accomplishing the task today. If you can, have them show you their process or how they are using their current product.

How do you know you have had a successful (year, month, day)?

This is a good question for business products, where you are trying to uncover metrics and customer goals. If your product can help your customer achieve their goals or help make them successful, you are well on your way to a valuable product.

How do you feel about (the current solution)?

This one is good for understanding opportunities to differentiate your product from competitors, especially during win-loss interviews. Good follow-up questions might be "Where does your current solution provide the most benefit? What do you like best about it?"

What is the most frustrating thing about (the current solution, a feature, your day, etc.)?

This is a great multi-purpose open-ended question that you can use to open up conversations and discover pain.

What do you wish you could do with (a product, a task, etc.) that you can't do today?

This is similar to "If you could wave a magic wand …

How would your (day, job, task) be different if you had this?

Variations of this question depending on the circumstances, but the objective is the same: understanding how your solution or feature solves a problem and what type of value a customer would place on solving that problem.

Can you give me an example?

This question provides you tangible evidence for your new product or feature.

Why would you recommend our solution (or us) to others?

You can use variations of this question to measure the satisfaction of your solution.

The live customer exchanges touch everyone, regardless of their function, in your organization. Exchanges such as the one described above calls upon people to work together to provide products and solutions to bring great experiences to your customers.

Following a customer exchange session, use the following questions to track progress and note the improvement in customer awareness, service and satisfaction. They do not cost anything and can pay off big time for customer results:

1. Did I do my best today to put the customer at the center of everything I do?
2. In what ways did our team take decisions that put the customer at the center of everything we do?
3. How did we manage our cross functional relationships so that the customer is at the center of everything we do?

There are varieties of initiatives that you can use to understand and sharpen the customer perspective in your business.

Here are four additional ideas to help put the customer at the center of everything you do:

1. **Place an empty chair in every meeting room in your company**. Reserve it for a customer of your choice. The empty chair helps remind everyone of where the customer is in your business.
2. **Use customer driven process design**. Are you ready to optimize and redesign core business processes? Imagine that you are a group of customers helping design your processes—what input would they have that would be helpful?

3. **Customer fish bowls** are helpful when you want to look at issues from another viewpoint, that being the customer perspective. The next time your leadership team is struggling with an important issue, take three or four leaders from the team and have them make a small circle and let them discuss the issue as if they were a group of customers. The other leaders form a larger circle around them (the customer fishbowl) and listen to the conversation. It is remarkable to hear the ideas and insights generated from the fishbowl format.
4. **Invite dissatisfied or exiting customers to lunch**. Keep a close eye on customers that choose to leave the business relationship with you. Invite them to lunch and hold a constructive and respectful customer-exit-interview. When managed correctly, you will gather a wealth of information and perhaps win your customer back.

Putting the customer at the center of everything you do is language that helps leadership teams tap into the common currency of purpose. Very few people really want to see customers fail. In fact, serving customers well is an implicit and explicit need, rarely exploited to its potential. I am yet to find an organization that says, "We are already doing everything possible to put the customer at the center of everything we do." In fact, the organizations that consistently rank high in customer care are the ones vigilantly looking for new opportunities to exceed their customers' expectations.

10.4 Signature Team Strengths

Executive ownershift is not intended to be a "complete make over" of your leadership team. Much of the work I do confirms or validates what is working well in your team. In every team and every organization, some things are working very well. Yet as all champions know, one cannot rest on the contentment of past successes.

Past victories are wonderful to cherish, yet it is the continued desire to improve and grow, the rigorous, systematic learning system you have in place and disciplined follow through that helps your team play at its best in the future. This means making the six touchstones of executive ownershift part of your signature team strengths.

Use the following questions to stimulate discussion and action that lead to growth and results for your leadership team:

1. **Resilient Relationships**

How well do we get non-material (unspoken concerns) on the table for constructive discussion in our team?
To what degree do I (and others in the team) direct frustration, disappointment, and critique to the person of origin or others?

How well do I proactively seek and give feedback to other members in our team?
Can and do I express my vulnerabilities to colleagues so they can help me?
How well do I understand the challenges of my colleagues and help them to be successful?

2. **Purposeful Practices**

Does our leadership team have an explicit purpose and have we shared that with our stakeholders?
Are we clear about our unique contribution to our business, focusing on those things that we can do?
How well have we exchanged best practice executive experiences and used these experiences to build our team charter or standards of excellence?
To what degree do we hold ourselves accountable to standards of excellence that we have created to ensure we strive to play at our best?
To what degree do we live by our purposeful practices and replicate this process to other teams throughout our business?

3. **Results Oriented Framework**

To what degree do we take time to provide feedback about our functional interfaces and individual interactions with each other?
Do we have an explicit set of guidelines that highlight how we communicate in face-to-face and virtual settings, as well as in written form?
How well do we take appropriate decisions and track the implementation of such decisions, via a decision score card, for example?
Do we walk the talk and insist on clarity and common understanding of roles and responsibilities in the leadership team and across the organization?
Do we, as a senior leadership team, focus on providing the future direction of our business and support for our people so they can create meaningful results that drive our business success?

4. **Make Meetings Matter**

Do we consistently prepare in advance for our meetings, physically through advice circulation of the agenda, as well as mental preparation?
To what degree do we drive decisions and create a culture of urgency through the way we meet?
Have we created a set of meeting guidelines that provide structure for our leadership meetings?
Do we have a system for continuous meeting improvement, a review session, at the end of each leadership meeting?
Can we say, as the executive team, that we run the best meeting in the company?

5. **Senseful Strategy**

To what degree have we created and communicated a clear and purposeful view of our organization in two or three years' time?
Have we created an open climate where people can share and discuss concerns, doubts and questions about our strategic topics and directions?
Are we actively benchmarking best practice collaborations and transforming collaborative bottlenecks and breakdowns?
How well do we practice "strategic quitting," that is letting go of initiatives that are not priorities or do not serve our strategic agenda?
How well and how often do customers serve as evangelists for the value that we bring to them and their business?

6. **Creating a Culture of Ownership**

To what degree are our conversations outcome driven, as compared to speaking simply about the activities we undertake?
How well do we encourage and take time for "why" conversations; those that help people understand the purpose and meaning of their work and our business?
Do people at different levels of our organization feel that they can challenge or question what they are asked to do, that is to "negotiate agreements" to a degree or are tasks seen as an "unquestionable order"?
To what degree does our leadership team strive to create the conditions for ownership, recognizing that a culture of ownership is something that people choose to do, and that delegation cannot be delegated?
Do we practice and insist on promise-based conversations, because we recognize that keeping promises strengthens trust in us and throughout our organization?

10.5 Know-Do-Want-Need

The mark of an effective leadership team is not determined by what they say, but rather by what and how they learn to engage others to create results.

Not everyone that reads this book will act upon what I have written. You can rationalize away why not now, why not to use it, why something will not work or that somebody else should do something to take you and your team off the hook. You may find temporary alternatives to ease the pain or to avoid the simple truth that leadership is highly personal and begins with each of us.

Some believe that intelligence and position represent that power of leadership. In my book, leadership is not about position, but about how we practice it, with our peers, our people and ourselves.

Through my observations and interactions with many leadership teams, the know-do-want-need dynamic serves as an important distinction of highly effective leadership teams, compared to leadership teams that just get by or struggle.

There is a great deal of wisdom at the executive level. So much, that at times leaders confuse knowing something with doing something, especially when it comes to doing things that relate to behavioral development on a personal or team level. Knowing something is not the same as doing something. Doing something, (new) requires courage, a willingness to fail, vulnerability and going first, all attributes of an executive ownershift leader. As long as I stay in the know, I can only direct others to do things that I am not demonstrating myself. To create the change we expect in others or our business, change begins with us and this means doing.

In Fig. 10.1, on the horizontal axis, on the left, we find "want to do" and on the right, we see "need to do." As long as my actions are driven by want to dos, there is a strong chance I remain in the comfort zone. When I do things that I see are needed by my team, my business, my customers and the market place, I am drawn into the stretch zone and new possibilities.

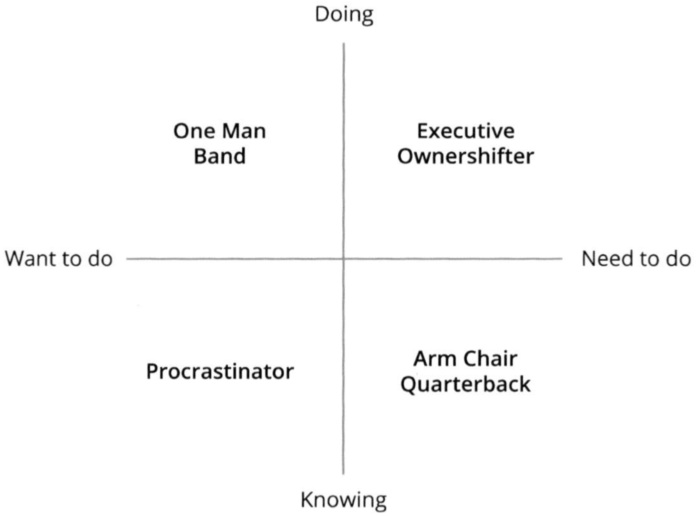

Fig. 10.1 The Know-Do-Want-Need quadrants

Doing things that need to be done, fulfilling the executive agenda are the behaviors of an executive ownershifter. When collectively practiced, you find a leadership team on their way to playing at their best.

The more successful we become, the more challenging it becomes to make changes for continuous improvement. Here are four ways executives can stimulate continuous improvement in their leadership teams:

1. Make a habit of addressing and reviewing **your fundamentals**.

What are the fundamentals of your leadership team success, your strategy, and your leadership culture? Watch any high performing team in any endeavor and we see that they consistently return and work on their fundaments.

2. Create real face time for meaningful dialog, problem solving and culture shaping.

Technology today gives us a wealth of opportunities to connect with each other; none is as effective as face-to-face encounters. Treat your face-to-face meetings as valuable moments of creation for your business.

3. Focus on the few things that make a difference

Exceptional leadership teams are clear about their mandate, shaped through their purposeful principles. They lead disciplined discussions and do not run down rabbit holes or drop down into the organization and play with other peoples' priorities.

4. Follow Through

Follow through ensures that things that should get done do get done. Delegation and strategic initiatives without watchful follow through rarely materialize into meaningful results.

Keep these 4Fs in mind and remember that your leadership team can be much better than it is today. This means you will run a better business as well.

There is no investment that you can make, not in brand marketing, not in process optimization, not in sales training, not in strategy, nor cultural change that can influence your organization quicker, and with more impact than to invest in the change, improvement, and growth of your leadership teams.

Executive Ownershift is not an exclusive secret for the C-Suite, to be practiced behind closed doors in a secret ceremony. It is an impactful social technology that starts with the senior leadership team and through personal ownership and example, it cascades through the entire organization.

Whether you contribute today in a leadership team, or aspire to do so in the future, or support leaders that cannot afford to play at less than their best, my intent throughout this book has been to help you make the very best of your executive ownershift.

Reference

1. https://en.wikipedia.org/wiki/Scared_Straight!.

Additional Resources

1. Garratt, B. (2003). *Thin on top, why corporate governance matters and how to measure and improve board performance*. Boston and London. Nicholas Brealey Publishing.
2. Goldsmith, M., & Reiter, M. (2015). *Triggers, creating behavior that lasts & becoming the person you want to be*. United States: Crown Business Publishing.
3. Guttman, H. M. (2008). *Great business teams, cracking the code for standout performance*. Canada and the United States: Wiley.
4. Hawkins, P. (Ed.). (2014). *Leadership team coaching in practice, developing high performance teams*. Great Britain and the United States: Kogan Page Limited.
5. Katzenbach, J. R., & Smith, D. K. (1993). *The wisdom of teams, creating the high performance organization*. United States: Harper Collins Publishers.

D. Norenberg, *Executive Ownershift*, Management for Professionals,
https://doi.org/10.1007/978-3-030-35828-0

Index

D. Norenberg, *Executive Ownershift*, Management for Professionals,
https://doi.org/10.1007/978-3-030-35828-0

Printed in Great Britain
by Amazon

0c808649-23f6-4416-bed4-490e6cd1c411R01